The Querist

Containing Several Queries Proposed to the
Consideration of the Public

by

George Berkeley

Part I

Query I.

Whether there ever was, is, or will be, an industrious nation poor, or an idle rich?

2. Qu. Whether a people can be called poor, where the common sort are well fed, clothed, and lodged?

3. Qu. Whether the drift and aim of every wise State should not be, to encourage industry in its members? And whether those who employ neither heads nor hands for the common benefit deserve not to be expelled like drones out of a well-governed State?

4. Qu. Whether the four elements, and man's labour therein, be not the true source of wealth?

5. Qu. Whether money be not only so far useful, as it stirreth up industry, enabling men mutually to participate the fruits of each other's labour?

6. Qu. Whether any other means, equally conducing to excite and circulate the industry of mankind, may not be as useful as money.

7. Qu. Whether the real end and aim of men be not power? And whether he who could have everything else at his wish or will would value money?

8. Qu. Whether the public aim in every well-govern'd State be not that each member, according to his just pretensions and industry, should have power?

9. Qu. Whether power be not referred to action; and whether action doth not follow appetite or will?

10. Qu. Whether fashion doth not create appetites; and whether the prevailing will of a nation is not the fashion?

11. Qu. Whether the current of industry and commerce be not determined by this prevailing will?

12. Qu. Whether it be not owing to custom that the fashions are agreeable?

13. Qu. Whether it may not concern the wisdom of the legislature to interpose in the making of fashions; and not leave an affair of so great influence to the management of women and fops, tailors and vintners?

14. Qu. Whether reasonable fashions are a greater restraint on freedom than those which are unreasonable?

15. Qu. Whether a general good taste in a people would not greatly conduce to their thriving? And whether an uneducated gentry be not the greatest of national evils?

16. Qu. Whether customs and fashions do not supply the place of reason in the vulgar of all ranks? Whether, therefore, it doth not very much import that they should be wisely framed?

17. Qu. Whether the imitating those neighbours in our fashions, to whom we bear no likeness in our circumstances, be not one cause of distress to this nation?

18. Qu. Whether frugal fashions in the upper rank, and comfortable living in the lower, be not the means to multiply inhabitants?

19. Qu. Whether the bulk of our Irish natives are not kept from thriving, by that cynical content in dirt and beggary which they possess to a degree beyond any other people in Christendom?

20. Qu. Whether the creating of wants be not the likeliest way to produce industry in a people? And whether, if our peasants were accustomed to eat beef and wear shoes, they would not be more industrious?

21. Qu. Whether other things being given, as climate, soil, etc., the wealth be not proportioned to the industry, and this to the circulation of credit, be the credit circulated or transferred by what marks or tokens soever?

22. Qu. Whether, therefore, less money swiftly circulating, be not, in effect, equivalent to more money slowly circulating? Or, whether, if the circulation be reciprocally as the quantity of coin, the nation can be a loser?

23. Qu. Whether money is to be considered as having an intrinsic value, or as being a commodity, a standard, a measure, or a pledge, as is variously suggested by writers? And whether the true idea of money, as such, be not altogether that of a ticket or counter?

24. Qu. Whether the value or price of things be not a compounded proportion, directly as the demand, and reciprocally as the plenty?

25. Qu. Whether the terms crown, livre, pound sterling, etc., are not to be considered as exponents or denominations of such proportion? And whether gold, silver, and paper are not tickets or counters for reckoning, recording, and transferring thereof?

26. Qu. Whether the denominations being retained, although the bullion were gone, things might not nevertheless be rated, bought, and sold, industry promoted, and a circulation of commerce maintained?

27. Qu. Whether an equal raising of all sorts of gold, silver, and copper coin can have any effect in bringing money into the

kingdom? And whether altering the proportions between the kingdom several sorts can have any other effect but multiplying one kind and lessening another, without any increase of the sum total?

28. Qu. Whether arbitrary changing the denomination of coin be not a public cheat?

29. Qu. Whether, nevertheless, the damage would be very considerable, if by degrees our money were brought back to the English value there to rest for ever?

30. Qu. Whether the English crown did not formerly pass with us for six shillings? And what inconvenience ensued to the public upon its reduction to the present value, and whether what hath been may not be?

31. Qu. What makes a wealthy people? Whether mines of gold and silver are capable of doing this? And whether the negroes, amidst the gold sands of Afric, are not poor and destitute?

32. Qu. Whether there be any vertue in gold or silver, other than as they set people at work, or create industry?

33. Qu. Whether it be not the opinion or will of the people, exciting them to industry, that truly enricheth a nation? And whether this doth not principally depend on the means for counting, transferring, and preserving power, that is, property of all kinds?

34. Qu. Whether if there was no silver or gold in the kingdom, our trade might not, nevertheless, supply bills of exchange, sufficient to answer the demands of absentees in England or elsewhere?

35. Qu. Whether current bank notes may not be deemed money? And whether they are not actually the greater part of the money of this kingdom?

36. Qu. Provided the wheels move, whether it is not the same thing, as to the effect of the machine, be this done by the force of wind, or water, or animals?

37. Qu. Whether power to command the industry of others be not real wealth? And whether money be not in truth tickets or tokens for conveying and recording such power, and whether it be of great consequence what materials the tickets are made of?

38. Qu. Whether trade, either foreign or domestic, be in truth any more than this commerce of industry?

39. Qu. Whether to promote, transfer, and secure this commerce, and this property in human labour, or, in other words, this power, be not the sole means of enriching a people, and how far this may be done independently of gold and silver?

40. Qu. Whether it were not wrong to suppose land itself to be wealth? And whether the industry of the people is not first to be consider'd, as that which constitutes wealth, which makes even land and silver to be wealth, neither of which would have, any value but as means and motives to industry?

41. Qu. Whether in the wastes of America a man might not possess twenty miles square of land, and yet want his dinner, or a coat to his back?

42. Qu. Whether a fertile land, and the industry of its inhabitants, would not prove inexhaustible funds of real wealth, be the counters for conveying and recording thereof what you will, paper, gold, or silver?

43. Qu. Whether a single hint be sufficient to overcome a prejudice? And whether even obvious truths will not sometimes bear repeating?

44. Qu. Whether, if human labour be the true source of wealth, it doth not follow that idleness should of all things be discouraged in a wise State?

45. Qu. Whether even gold or silver, if they should lessen the industry of its inhabitants, would not be ruinous to a country? And whether Spain be not an instance of this?

46. Qu. Whether the opinion of men, and their industry consequent thereupon, be not the true wealth of Holland and not the silver supposed to be deposited in the bank at Amsterdam?

47. Qu. Whether there is in truth any such treasure lying dead? And whether it be of great consequence to the public that it should be real rather than notional?

48. Qu. Whether in order to understand the true nature of wealth and commerce, it would not be right to consider a ship's crew cast upon a desert island, and by degrees forming themselves to business and civil life, while industry begot credit, and credit moved to industry?

49. Qu. Whether such men would not all set themselves to work? Whether they would not subsist by the mutual participation of each other's industry? Whether, when one man had in his way procured more than he could consume, he would not exchange his superfluities to supply his wants? Whether this must not produce credit? Whether, to facilitate these conveyances, to record and circulate this credit, they would not soon agree on certain tallies, tokens, tickets, or counters?

50. Qu. Whether reflection in the better sort might not soon remedy our evils? And whether our real defect be not a wrong way of thinking?

51. Qu. Whether it would not be an unhappy turn in our gentlemen, if they should take more thought to create an interest to themselves in this or that county, or borough, than to promote the real interest of their country?

52. Qu. Whether it be not a bull to call that making an interest, whereby a man spendeth much and gaineth nothing?

53. Qu. Whether if a man builds a house he doth not in the first place provide a plan which governs his work? And shall the pubic act without an end, a view, a plan?

54. Qu. Whether by how much the less particular folk think for themselves, the public be not so much the more obliged to think for them?

55. Qu. Whether cunning be not one thing and good sense another? and whether a cunning tradesman doth not stand in his own light?

56. Qu. Whether small gains be not the way to great profit? And if our tradesmen are beggars, whether they may not thank themselves for it?

57. Qu. Whether some way might not be found for making criminals useful in public works, instead of sending them either to America, or to the other world?

58. Qu. Whether we may not, as well as other nations, contrive employment for them? And whether servitude, chains, and hard labour, for a term of years, would not be a more discouraging as

well as a more adequate punishment for felons than even death itself?

59. Qu. Whether there are not such things in Holland as bettering houses for bringing young gentlemen to order? And whether such an institution would be useless among us?

60. Qu. Whether it be true that the poor in Holland have no resource but their own labour, and yet there are no beggars in their streets?

61. Qu. Whether he whose luxury consumeth foreign products, and whose industry produceth nothing domestic to exchange for them, is not so far forth injurious to his country?

62. Qu. Whether, consequently, the fine gentlemen, whose employment is only to dress, drink, and play, be not a pubic nuisance?

63. Qu. Whether necessity is not to be hearkened to before convenience, and convenience before luxury?

64. Qu. Whether to provide plentifully for the poor be not feeding the root, the substance whereof will shoot upwards into the branches, and cause the top to flourish?

65. Qu. Whether there be any instance of a State wherein the people, living neatly and plentifully, did not aspire to wealth?

66. Qu. Whether nastiness and beggary do not, on the contrary, extinguish all such ambition, making men listless, hopeless, and slothful?

67. Qu. Whether a country inhabited by people well fed, clothed and lodged would not become every day more populous? And whether a numerous stock of people in such circumstances would?

and how far the product of not constitute a flourishing nation; our own country may suffice for the compassing of this end?

68. Qu. Whether a people who had provided themselves with the necessaries of life in good plenty would not soon extend their industry to new arts and new branches of commerce?

69. Qu. Whether those same manufactures which England imports from other countries may not be admitted from Ireland? And, if so, whether lace, carpets, and tapestry, three considerable articles of English importation, might not find encouragement in Ireland? And whether an academy for design might not greatly conduce to the perfecting those manufactures among us?

70. Qu. Whether France and Flanders could have drawn so much money from England for figured silks, lace, and tapestry, if they had not had academies for designing?

71. Qu. Whether, when a room was once prepared, and models in plaster of Paris, the annual expense of such an academy need stand the pubic in above two hundred pounds a year?

72. Qu. Whether our linen-manufacture would not find the benefit of this institution? And whether there be anything that makes us fall short of the Dutch in damasks, diapers, and printed linen, but our ignorance in design?

73. Qu. Whether those specimens of our own manufacture, hung up in a certain public place, do not sufficiently declare such our ignorance? and whether for the honour of the nation they ought not to be removed?

74. Qu. Whether those who may slight this affair as notional have sufficiently considered the extensive use of the art of design, and its influence in most trades and manufactures, wherein the forms of things are often more regarded than the materials?

75. Qu. Whether there be any art sooner learned than that of making carpets? And whether our women, with little time and pains, may not make more beautiful carpets than those imported from Turkey? And whether this branch of the woollen manufacture be not open to us?

76. Qu. Whether human industry can produce, from such cheap materials, a manufacture of so great value by any other art as by those of sculpture and painting?

77. Qu. Whether pictures and statues are not in fact so much treasure? And whether Rome and Florence would not be poor towns without them?

78. Qu. Whether they do not bring ready money as well as jewels? Whether in Italy debts are not paid, and children portioned with them, as with gold and silver?

79. Qu. Whether it would not be more prudent, to strike out and exert ourselves in permitted branches of trade, than to fold our hands, and repine that we are not allowed the woollen?

80. Qu. Whether it be true that two millions are yearly expended by England in foreign lace and linen?

81. Qu. Whether immense sums are not drawn yearly into the Northern countries, for supplying the British navy with hempen manufactures?

82. Qu. Whether there be anything more profitable than. hemp? And whether there should not be great premiums for encouraging our hempen trade? What advantages may not Great Britain make of a country where land and labour are so cheap?

83. Qu. Whether Ireland alone might not raise hemp sufficient for the British navy? And whether it would not be vain to expect

this from the British Colonies in America, where hands are so scarce, and labour so excessively dear?

84. Qu. Whether, if our own people want will or capacity for such an attempt, it might not be worth while for some undertaking spirits in England to make settlements, and raise hemp in the counties of Clare and Limerick, than which, perhaps, there is not fitter land in the world for that purpose? And whether both nations would not find their advantage therein?

85. Qu. Whether if all the idle hands in this kingdom were employed on hemp and flax, we might not find sufficient vent for these manufactures?

86. Qu. How far it may be in our own power to better our affairs, without interfering with our neighbours?

87. Qu. Whether the prohibition of our woollen trade ought not naturally to put us on other methods which give no jealousy?

88. Qu. Whether paper be not a valuable article of commerce? And whether it be not true that one single bookseller in London yearly expended above four thousand pounds in that foreign commodity?

89. Qu. How it comes to pass that the Venetians and Genoese, who wear so much less linen, and so much worse than we do, should yet make very good paper, and in great quantity, while we make very little?

90. Qu. How long it will be before my countrymen find out that it is worth while to spend a penny in order to get a groat?

91. Qu. If all the land were tilled that is fit for tillage, and all that sowed with hemp and flax that is fit for raising them, whether we

should have much sheep-walk beyond what was sufficient to supply the necessities of the kingdom?

92. Qu. Whether other countries have not flourished without the woollen trade?

93. Qu. Whether it be not a sure sign or effect of a country's inhabitants? And, thriving, to see it well cultivated and full of; if so, whether a great quantity of sheep-walk be not ruinous to a country, rendering it waste and thinly inhabited?

94. Qu. Whether the employing so much of our land under sheep be not in fact an Irish blunder?

95. Qu. Whether our hankering after our woollen trade be not the true and only reason which hath created a jealousy in England towards Ireland? And whether anything can hurt us more than such jealousy?

96. Qu. Whether it be not the true interest of both nations to become one people? And whether either be sufficiently apprised of this?

97. Qu. Whether the upper part of this people are not truly English, by blood, language, religion, manners, inclination, and interest?

98. Qu. Whether we are not as much Englishmen as the children of old Romans, born in Britain, were still Romans?

99. Qu. Whether it be not our true interest not to interfere with them; and, in every other case, whether it be not their true interest to befriend us?

100. Qu. Whether a mint in Ireland might not be of great convenience to the kingdom; and whether it could be attended

with any possible inconvenience to Great Britain? And whether there were not mints in Naples and Sicily, when those kingdoms were provinces to Spain or the house of Austria?

101. Qu. Whether anything can be more ridiculous than for the north of Ireland to be jealous of a linen manufacturer in the south?

102. Qu. Whether the county of Tipperary be not much better land than the county of Armagh; and yet whether the latter is not much better improved and inhabited than the former?

103. Qu. Whether every landlord in the kingdom doth not know the cause of this? And yet how few are the better for such their knowledge?

104. Qu. Whether large farms under few hands, or small ones under many, are likely to be made most of? And whether flax and tillage do not naturally multiply hands, and divide land into small holdings, and well-improved?

105. Qu. Whether, as our exports are lessened, we ought not to lessen our imports? And whether these will not be lessened as our demands, and these as our wants, and these as our customs or fashions? Of how great consequence therefore are fashions to the public?

106. Qu. Whether it would not be more reasonable to mend our state than to complain of it; and how far this may be in our own power?

107. Qu. What the nation gains by those who live in Ireland upon the produce of foreign Countries?

108. Qu. How far the vanity of our ladies in dressing, and of our gentlemen in drinking, contributes to the general misery of the people?

109. Qu. Whether nations, as wise and opulent as ours, have not made sumptuary laws; and what hinders us from doing the same?

110. Qu. Whether those who drink foreign liquors, and deck themselves and their families with foreign ornaments, are not so far forth to be reckoned absentees?

111. Qu. Whether, as our trade is limited, we ought not to limit our expenses; and whether this be not the natural and obvious remedy?

112. Qu. Whether the dirt, and famine, and nakedness of the bulk of our people might not be remedied, even although we had no foreign trade? And whether this should not be our first care; and whether, if this were once provided for, the conveniences of the rich would not soon follow?

113. Qu. Whether comfortable living doth not produce wants, and wants industry, and industry wealth?

114. Qu. Whether there is not a great difference between Holland and Ireland? And whether foreign commerce, without which the one could not subsist, be so necessary for the other?

115. Qu. Might we not put a hand to the plough, or the spade, although we had no foreign commerce?

116. Qu. Whether the exigencies of nature are not to be answered by industry on our own soil? And how far the conveniences and comforts of life may be procured by a domestic commerce between the several parts of this kingdom?

117. Qu. Whether the women may not sew, spin, weave, embroider sufficiently for the embellishment of their persons, and even enough to raise envy in each other, without being beholden to foreign countries?

118. Qu. Suppose the bulk of our inhabitants had shoes to their feet, clothes to their backs, and beef in their bellies, might not such a state be eligible for the public, even though the squires were condemned to drink ale and cider?

119. Qu. Whether, if drunkenness be a necessary evil, men may not as well drink the growth of their own country?

120. Qu. Whether a nation within itself might not have real wealth, sufficient to give its inhabitants power and distinction, without the help of gold and silver?

121. Qu. Whether, if the arts of sculpture and painting were encouraged among us, we might not furnish our houses in a much nobler manner with our own manufactures?

122. Qu. Whether we have not, or may not have, all the necessary materials for building at home?

123. Qu. Whether tiles and plaster may not supply the place of Norway fir for flooring and wainscot?

124. Qu. Whether plaster be not warmer, as well as more secure, than deal? And whether a modern fashionable house, lined with fir, daubed over with oil and paint, be not like a fire-ship, ready to be lighted up by all accidents?

125. Qu. Whether larger houses, better built and furnished, a greater train of servants, the difference with regard to equipage and table between finer and coarser, more and less elegant, may not be sufficient to feed a reasonable share of vanity, or support

all proper distinctions? And whether all these may not be procured by domestic industry out of the four elements, without ransacking the four quarters of the globe?

126. Qu. Whether anything is a nobler ornament, in the eye of the world, than an Italian palace, that is, stone and mortar skilfully put together, and adorned with sculpture and painting; and whether this may not be compassed without foreign trade?

127. Qu. Whether an expense in gardens and plantations would not be an elegant distinction for the rich, a domestic magnificence employing many hands within, and drawing nothing from abroad?

128. Qu. Whether the apology which is made for foreign luxury in England, to wit, that they could not carry on their trade without imports as well as exports, will hold in Ireland?

129. Qu. Whether one may not be allowed to conceive and suppose a society or nation of human creatures, clad in woollen cloths and stuffs, eating good bread, beef and mutton, poultry and fish, in great plenty, drinking ale, mead, and cider, inhabiting decent houses built of brick and marble, taking their pleasure in fair parks and gardens, depending on no foreign imports either for food or raiment? And whether such people ought much to be pitied?

130. Qu. Whether Ireland be not as well qualified for such a state as any nation under the sun?

131. Qu. Whether in such a state the inhabitants may not contrive to pass the twenty-four hours with tolerable ease and cheerfulness? And whether any people upon earth can do more?

132. Qu. Whether they may not eat, drink, play, dress, visit, sleep in good beds, sit by good fires, build, plant, raise a name, make estates, and spend them?

133. Qu. Whether, upon the whole, a domestic trade may not suffice in such a country as Ireland, to nourish and clothe its inhabitants, and provide them with the reasonable conveniences and even comforts of life?

134. Qu. Whether a general habit of living well would not produce numbers and industry' and whether, considering the tendency of human kind, the consequence thereof would not be foreign trade and riches, how unnecessary soever?

135. Qu. Whether, nevertheless, it be a crime to inquire how far we may do without foreign trade, and what would follow on such a supposition?

136. Qu. Whether the number and welfare of the subjects be not the true strength of the crown?

137. Qu. Whether in all public institutions there should not be an end proposed, which is to be the rule and limit of the means? Whether this end should not be the well-being of the whole? And whether, in order to this, the first step should not be to clothe and feed our people?

138. Qu. Whether there be upon earth any Christian or civilized people so beggarly, wretched, and destitute as the common Irish?

139. Qu. Whether, nevertheless, there is any other people whose wants may be more easily supplied from home?

140. Qu. Whether, if there was a wall of brass a thousand cubits high round this kingdom, our natives might not nevertheless live cleanly and comfortably, till the land, and reap the fruits of it?

141. Qu. What should hinder us from exerting ourselves, using our hands and brains, doing something or other, man, woman, and child, like the other inhabitants of God's earth?

142. Qu. Be the restraining our trade well or ill advised in our neighbours, with respect to their own interest, yet whether it be not plainly ours to accommodate ourselves to it?

143. Qu. Whether it be not vain to think of persuading other people to see their interest, while we continue blind to our own?

144. Qu. Whether there be any other nation possess'd of so much good land, and so many able hands to work it, which yet is beholden for bread to foreign countries?

145. Qu. Whether it be true that we import corn to the value of two hundred thousand pounds in some years?

146. Qu. Whether we are not undone by fashions made for other people? And whether it be not madness in a poor nation to imitate a rich one?

147. Qu. Whether a woman of fashion ought not to be declared a public enemy?

148. Qu. Whether it be not certain that from the single town of Cork were exported, in one year, no less than one hundred and seven thousand one hundred and sixty-one barrels of beef; seven thousand three hundred and seventy-nine barrels of pork; thirteen thousand four hundred and sixty-one casks, and eighty-five thousand seven hundred and twenty-seven firkins of butter? And what hands were employed in this manufacture?

149. Qu. Whether a foreigner could imagine that one half of the people were starving, in a country which sent out such plenty of provisions?

150. Qu. Whether an Irish lady, set out with French silks and Flanders lace, may not be said to consume more beef and butter than a hundred of our labouring peasants?

151. Qu. Whether nine-tenths of our foreign trade be not carried on singly to support the article of vanity?

152. Qu. Whether it can be hoped that private persons will not indulge this folly, unless restrained by the public?

153. Qu. How vanity is maintained in other countries? Whether in Hungary, for instance, a proud nobility are not subsisted with small imports from abroad?

154. Qu. Whether there be a prouder people upon earth than the noble Venetians, although they all wear plain black clothes?

155. Qu. Whether a people are to be pitied that will not sacrifice their little particular vanities to the public. good? And yet, whether each part would not except their own foible from this public sacrifice, the squire his bottle, the lady her lace?

156. Qu. Whether claret be not often drank rather for vanity than for health, or pleasure?

157. Qu. Whether it be true that men of nice palates have been imposed on, by elder wine for French claret, and by mead for palm sack?

158. Qu. Do not Englishmen abroad purchase beer and cider at ten times the price of wine?

159. Qu. How many gentlemen are there in England of a thousand pounds per annum who never drink wine in their own houses? Whether the same may be said of any in Ireland who have even? one hundred pounds per annum.

160. Qu. What reasons have our neighbours in England for discouraging French wines which may not hold with respect to us also?

161. Qu. How much of the necessary sustenance of our people is yearly exported for brandy?

162. Qu. Whether, if people must poison themselves, they had not better do it with their own growth?

163. Qu. If we imported neither claret from France, nor fir from Norway, what the nation would save by it?

164. Qu. When the root yieldeth insufficient nourishment, whether men do not top the tree to make the lower branches thrive?

165. Qu. Whether, if our ladies drank sage or balm tea out of Irish ware, it would be an insupportable national calamity?

166. Qu. Whether it be really true that such wine is best as most encourages drinking, i.e., that must be given in the largest dose to produce its effect? And whether this holds with regard to any other medicine?

167. Qu. Whether that trade should not be accounted most pernicious wherein the balance is most against us? And whether this be not the trade with France?

168. Qu. Whether it be not even madness to encourage trade with a nation that takes nothing of our manufacture?

169. Qu. Whether Ireland can hope to thrive if the major part of her patriots shall be found in the French interest?

170. Qu. Why, if a bribe by the palate or the purse be in effect the same thing, they should not be alike infamous?

171. Qu. Whether the vanity and luxury of a few ought to stand in competition with the interest of a nation?

172. Qu. Whether national wants ought not to be the rule of trade? And whether the most pressing wants of. the majority ought not to be first consider'd?

173. Qu. Whether it is possible the country should be well improved, while our beef is exported, and our labourers live upon potatoes?

174. Qu. If it be resolved that we cannot do without foreign trade, whether, at least, it may not be worth while to consider what branches thereof deserve to be entertained, and how far we may be able to carry it on under our present limitations?

175. Qu. What foreign imports may be necessary for clothing and feeding the families of persons not worth above one hundred pounds a year? And how many wealthier there are in the kingdom, and what proportion they bear to the other inhabitants?

176. Qu. Whether trade be not then on a right foot, when foreign commodities are imported in exchange only for domestic superfluities?

177. Qu. Whether the quantities of beef, butter, wool, and leather, exported from this island, can be reckoned the superfluities of a country, where there are so many natives naked and famished?

178. Qu. Whether it would not be wise so to order our trade as to export manufactures rather than provisions, and of those such as employ most hands?

179. Qu. Whether she would not be a very vile matron, and justly thought either mad or foolish, that should give away the necessaries of life from her naked and famished children, in exchange for pearls to stick in her hair, and sweetmeats to please her own palate?

180. Qu. Whether a nation might not be consider'd as a family?

181. Qu. Whether other methods may not be found for supplying the funds, besides the custom on things imported?

182. Qu. Whether any art or manufacture be so difficult as the making of good laws?

183. Qu. Whether our peers and gentlemen are born legislators? Or, whether that faculty be acquired by study and reflection?

184. Qu. Whether to comprehend the real interest of a people, and the means to procure it, doth not imply some fund of knowledge, historical, moral, and political, with a faculty of reason improved by learning?

185. Qu. Whether every enemy to learning be not a Goth? And whether every such Goth among us be not an enemy to the country?

186. Qu. Whether, therefore, it would not be an omen of ill presage, a dreadful phenomenon in the land, if our great men should take it in their heads to deride learning and education?

187. Qu. Whether, on the contrary, it should not seem worth while to erect a mart of literature in this kingdom, under wiser regulations and better discipline than in any other part of Europe? And whether this would not be an infallible means of drawing men and money into the kingdom?

188. Qu. Whether the governed be not too numerous for the governing part of our college? And whether it might not be expedient to convert thirty natives-places into twenty fellowships?

189. Qu. Whether, if we had two colleges, there might not spring a useful emulation between them? And whether it might not be

contrived so to divide the fellows, scholars, and revenues between both, as that no member should be a loser thereby?

190. Qu. Whether ten thousand pounds well laid out might not build a decent college, fit to contain two hundred persons; and whether the purchase money of the chambers would not go a good way towards defraying the expense?

191. Qu. Where this college should be situated?

192. Qu. Whether it is possible a State should not thrive, whereof the lower part were industrious, and the upper wise?

193. Qu. Whether the collected wisdom of ages and nations be not found in books, improved and applied by study?

194. Qu. Whether it was not an Irish professor who first opened the public schools at Oxford? Whether this island hath not been anciently famous for learning? And whether at this day it hath any better chance for being considerable?

195. Qu. Whether we may not with better grace sit down and complain, when we have done all that lies in our power to help ourselves?

196. Qu. Whether the gentleman of estate hath a right to be idle; and whether he ought not to be the great promoter and director of industry among his tenants and neighbours?

197. Qu. Whether the real foundation for wealth must not be laid in the numbers, the frugality, and the industry of the people? And whether all attempts to enrich a nation by other means, as raising the coin, stock-jobbing, and such arts are not vain?

198. Qu. Whether a door ought not to be shut against all other methods of growing rich, save only by industry and. merit? And whether wealth got otherwise would not be ruinous to the public?

199. Qu. Whether the abuse of banks and paper-money is a just objection against the use thereof? And whether such abuse might not easily be prevented?

200. Qu. Whether national banks are not found useful in Venice, Holland, and Hamburg? And whether it is not possible to contrive one that may be useful also in Ireland?

201. Qu. Whether any nation ever was in greater want of such an expedient than Ireland?

202. Qu. Whether the banks of Venice and Amsterdam are not in the hands of the public?

203. Qu. Whether it may not be worth while to inform ourselves in the nature of those banks? And what reason can be assigned why Ireland should not reap the benefit of such public banks as well as other countries?

204. Qu. Whether a bank of national credit, supported by public funds and secured by Parliament, be a chimera or impossible thing? And if not, what would follow from the supposal of such a bank?

205. Qu. Whether the currency of a credit so well secured would not be of great advantage to our trade and manufactures?

206. Qu. Whether the notes of such public bank would not have a more general circulation than those of private banks, as being less subject to frauds and hazards?

207. Qu. Whether it be not agreed that paper hath in many respects the advantage above coin, as being of more dispatch in payments, more easily transferred, preserved, and recovered when lost?

208. Qu. Whether, besides these advantages, there be not an evident necessity for circulating credit by paper, from the defect of coin in this kingdom?

209. Qu. Whether the public may not as well save the interest which it now pays?

210. Qu. What would happen if two of our banks should break at once? And whether it be wise to neglect providing against an event which experience hath shewn us not to be impossible?

211. Qu. Whether such an accident would not particularly affect the bankers? And therefore whether a national bank would not be a security even to private bankers?

212. Qu. Whether we may not easily avoid the inconveniencies attending the paper-money of New England, which were incurred by their issuing too great a quantity of notes, by their having no silver in bank to exchange for notes, by their not insisting upon repayment of the loans at the time prefixed, and especially by their want of manufactures to answer their imports from Europe?

213. Qu. Whether a combination of bankers might not do wonders, and whether bankers know their own strength?

214. Qu. Whether a bank in private hands might not even overturn a government? and whether this was not the case of the Bank of St. George in Genoa? [Footnote: See the Vindication and Advancement of our national Constitution and Credit. Printed in London 1710.]

215. Qu. Whether we may not easily prevent the ill effects of such a bank as Mr Law proposed for Scotland, which was faulty in not limiting the quantum of bills, and permitting all persons to take out what bills they pleased, upon the mortgage of lands, whence by a glut of paper, the prices of things must rise? Whence also the fortunes of men must increase in denomination, though not in value; whence pride, idleness, and beggary?

216. Qu. Whether such banks as those of England and Scotland might not be attended with great inconveniences, as lodging too much power in the hands of private men, and giving handle for monopolies, stock-jobbing, and destructive schemes?

217. Qu. Whether the national bank, projected by an anonymous writer in the latter end of Queen Anne's reign, might not on the other hand be attended with as great inconveniencies by lodging too much power in the Government?

218. Qu. Whether the bank projected by Murray, though it partake, in many useful particulars, with that of Amsterdam, yet, as it placeth too great power in the hands of a private society, might not be dangerous to the public?

219. Qu. Whether it be rightly remarked by some that, as banking brings no treasure into the kingdom like trade, private wealth must sink as the bank riseth? And whether whatever causeth industry to flourish and circulate may not be said to increase our treasure?

220. Qu. Whether the ruinous effects of Mississippi, South Sea, and such schemes were not owing to an abuse of paper money or credit, in making it a means for idleness and gaming, instead of a motive and help to industry?

221. Qu. Whether those effects could have happened had there been no stock-jobbing? And whether stock-jobbing could at first

have been set on foot, without an imaginary foundation of some improvement to the stock by trade? Whether, therefore, when there are no such prospects, or cheats, or private schemes proposed, the same effects can be justly feared?

222. Qu. Whether by a national bank, be not properly understood a bank, not only established by public authority as the Bank of England, but a bank in the hands of the public, wherein there are no shares: whereof the public alone is proprietor, and reaps all the benefit?

223. Qu. Whether, having considered the conveniencies of banking and paper-credit in some countries, and the inconveniencies thereof in others, we may not contrive to adopt the former, and avoid the latter?

224. Qu. Whether great evils, to which other schemes are liable, may not be prevented, by excluding the managers of the bank from a share in the legislature?

225. Qu. Whether the rise of the bank of Amsterdam was not purely casual, for the security and dispatch of payments? And whether the good effects thereof, in supplying the place of coin, and promoting a ready circulation of industry and commerce may not be a lesson to us, to do that by design which others fell upon by chance?

226. Qu. Whether the bank proposed to be established in Ireland, under the notion of a national bank, by the voluntary subscription of three hundred thousand pounds, to pay off the national debt, the interest of which sum to be paid the subscribers, subject to certain terms of redemption, be not in reality a private bank, as those of England and Scotland, which are national only in name, being in the hands of particular persons, and making dividends on the money paid in by

subscribers? [Footnote: See a Proposal for the Relief of Ireland, &c. Printed in Dublin A. D. 1734]

227. Qu. Whether plenty of small cash be not absolutely necessary for keeping up a circulation among the people; that is, whether copper be not more necessary than gold?

228. Qu. Whether it is not worth while to reflect on the expedients made use of by other nations, paper-money, bank-notes, public funds, and credit in all its shapes, to examine what hath been done and devised to add to our own animadversions, and upon the whole offer such hints as seem not unworthy the attention of the public?

229. Qu. Whether that, which increaseth the stock of a nation be not a means of increasing its trade? And whether that which increaseth the current credit of a nation may not be said to increase its stock?

230. Qu. Whether it may not be expedient to appoint certain funds or stock for a national bank, under direction of certain persons, one-third whereof to be named by the Government, and one-third by each House of Parliament?

231. Qu. Whether the directors should not be excluded from sitting in either House, and whether they should not be subject to the audit and visitation of a standing committee of both Houses?

232. Qu. Whether such committee of inspectors should not be changed every two years, one-half going out, and another coming in by ballot?

233. Qu. Whether the notes ought not to be issued in lots, to be let at interest on mortgaged lands, the whole number of lots to be divided among the four provinces, rateably to the number of hearths in each?

234. Qu. Whether it may not be expedient to appoint four counting-houses, one in each province, for converting notes into specie?

235. Qu. Whether a limit should not be fixed, which no person might exceed, in taking out notes?

236. Qu. Whether, the better to answer domestic circulation, it may not be right to issue notes as low as twenty shillings?

237. Qu. Whether all the bills should be issued at once, or rather by degrees, that so men may be gradually accustomed and reconciled to the bank?

238. Qu. Whether the keeping of the cash, and the direction of the bank, ought not to be in different hands, and both under public control?

239. Qu. Whether the same rule should not alway be observed, of lending out money or notes, only to half the value of the mortgaged land? and whether this value should not alway be rated at the same number of years' purchase as at first?

240. Qu. Whether care should not be taken to prevent an undue rise of the value of land?

241. Qu. Whether the increase of industry and people will not of course raise the value of land? And whether this rise may not be sufficient?

242. Qu. Whether land may not be apt to rise on the issuing too great plenty of notes?

243. Qu. Whether this may not be prevented by the gradual and slow issuing of notes, and by frequent sales of lands?

244. Qu. Whether interest doth not measure the true value of land; for instance, where money is at five per cent, whether land is not worth twenty years' purchase?

245. Qu. Whether too small a proportion of money would not hurt the landed man, and too great a proportion the monied man? And whether the quantum of notes ought not to bear proportion to the pubic demand? And whether trial must not shew what this demand will be?

246. Qu. Whether the exceeding this measure might not produce divers bad effects, one whereof would be the loss of our silver?

247. Qu. Whether interest paid into the bank ought not to go on augmenting its stock?

248. Qu. Whether it would or would not be right to appoint that the said interest be paid in notes only?

249. Qu. Whether the notes of this national bank should not be received in all payments into the exchequer?

250. Qu. Whether on supposition that the specie should fail, the credit would not, nevertheless, still pass, being admitted in all payments of the public revenue?

251. Qu. Whether the pubic can become bankrupt so long as the notes are issued on good security?

252. Qu. Whether mismanagement, prodigal living, hazards by trade, which often affect private banks, are equally to be apprehended in a pubic one?

253. Qu. Whether as credit became current, and this raised the value of land, the security must not of course rise?

254. Qu. Whether, as our current domestic credit grew, industry would not grow likewise; and if industry, our manufactures; and if these, our foreign credit?

255. Qu. Whether by degrees, as business and people multiplied, more bills may not be issued, without augmenting the capital stock, provided still, that they are issued on good security; which further issuing of new bills, not to be without consent of Parliament?

256. Qu. Whether such bank would not be secure? Whether the profits accruing to the pubic would not be very considerable? And whether industry in private persons would not be supplied, and a general circulation encouraged?

257. Qu. Whether such bank should, or should not, be allowed to issue notes for money deposited therein? And, if not, whether the bankers would have cause to complain?

258. Qu. Whether, if the public thrives, all particular persons must not feel the benefit thereof, even the bankers themselves?

259. Qu. Whether, beside the Bank–Company, there are not in England many private wealthy bankers, and whether they were more before the erecting of that company?

260. Qu. Whether as industry increased, our manufactures would not flourish; and as these flourished, whether better returns would not be made from estates to their landlords, both within and without the kingdom?

261. Qu. Whether we have not paper-money circulating among, whether, therefore, we might not as well have that us already which is secured by the public, and whereof the pubic reaps the benefit?

262. Qu. Whether there are not two general ways of circulating money, to wit, play and traffic? and whether stock-jobbing is not to be ranked under the former?

263. Qu. Whether there are more than two things that might draw silver out of the bank, when its credit was once well established, to wit, foreign demands and small payments at home?

264. Qu. Whether, if our trade with France were checked, the former of these causes could be supposed to operate at all? and whether the latter could operate to any great degree?

265. Qu. Whether the sure way to supply people with tools and materials, and to set them at work, be not a free circulation of money, whether silver or paper?

266. Qu. Whether in New England all trade and business is not as much at a stand, upon a scarcity of paper-money, as with us from the want of specie?

267. Qu. Whether paper-money or notes may not be issued from the national bank, on the security of hemp, of linen, or other manufactures whereby the poor might be supported in their industry?

268. Qu. Whether it be certain that the quantity of silver in the bank of Amsterdam be greater now than at first; but whether it be not certain that there is a greater circulation of industry and extent of trade, more people, ships, houses, and commodities of all sorts, more power by sea and land?

269. Qu. Whether money, lying dead in the bank of Amsterdam, would not be as useless as in the mine?

270. Qu. Whether our visible security in land could be doubted? And whether there be anything like this in the bank of Amsterdam?

271. Qu. Whether it be just to apprehend danger from trusting a national bank with power to extend its credit, to circulate notes which it shall be felony to counterfeit, to receive goods on loans, to purchase lands, to sell also or alienate them, and to deal in bills of exchange; when these powers are no other than have been trusted for many years with the bank of England, although in truth but a private bank?

272. Qu. Whether the objection from monopolies and an overgrowth of power, which are made against private banks, can possibly hold against a national one?

273. Qu. Whether banks raised by private subscription would be as advantageous to the public as to the subscribers? and whether risks and frauds might not be more justly apprehended from them?

274. Qu. Whether the evil effects which of late years have attended paper-money and credit in Europe did not spring from subscriptions, shares, dividends, and stock-jobbing?

275. Qu. Whether the great evils attending paper-money in the British Plantations of America have not sprung from the overrating their lands, and issuing paper without discretion, and from the legislators breaking their own rules in favour of themselves, thus sacrificing the public to their private benefit? And whether a little sense and honesty might not easily prevent all such inconveniences?

276. Qu. Whether an argument from the abuse of things, against the use of them, be conclusive?

277. Qu. Whether he who is bred to a part be fitted to judge of the whole?

278. Qu. Whether interest be not apt to bias judgment? and whether traders only are to be consulted about trade, or bankers about money?

279. Qu. Whether the subject of Freethinking in religion be not exhausted? And whether it be not high time for our freethinkers to turn their thoughts to the improvement of their country?

280. Qu. Whether any man hath a right to judge, that will not be at the pains to distinguish?

281. Qu. Whether there be not a wide difference between the profits going to augment the national stock, and being divided among private sharers? And whether, in the former case, there can possibly be any gaming or stock-jobbing?

282. Qu. Whether it must not be ruinous for a nation to sit down to game, be it with silver or with paper?

283. Qu. Whether, therefore, the circulating paper, in the late ruinous schemes of France and England, was the true evil, and not rather the circulating thereof without industry? And whether the bank of Amsterdam, where industry had been for so many years subsisted and circulated by transfers on paper, doth not clearly decide this point?

284. Qu. Whether there are not to be seen in America fair towns, wherein the people are well lodged, fed, and clothed, without a beggar in their streets, although there be not one grain of gold or silver current among them?

285. Qu. Whether these people do not exercise all arts and trades, build ships and navigate them to all parts of the world, purchase

lands, till and reap the fruits of them, buy and sell, educate and provide for their children? Whether they do not even indulge themselves in foreign vanities?

286. Qu. Whether, whatever inconveniences those people may have incurred from not observing either rules or bounds in their paper money, yet it be not certain that they are in a more flourishing condition, have larger and better built towns, more plenty, more industry, more arts and civility, and a more extensive commerce, than when they had gold and silver current among them?

287. Qu. Whether a view of the ruinous effects of absurd schemes and credit mismanaged, so as to produce gaming and madness instead of industry, can be any just objection against a national bank calculated purely to promote industry?

288. Qu. Whether a scheme for the welfare of this nation should not take in the whole inhabitants? And whether it be not a vain attempt, to project the flourishing of our Protestant gentry, exclusive of the bulk of the natives?

289. Qu. Whether, therefore, it doth not greatly concern the State, that our Irish natives should be converted, and the whole nation united in the same religion, the same allegiance, and the same interest? and how this may most probably be effected?

290. Qu. Whether an oath, testifying allegiance to the king, and disclaiming the pope's authority in temporals, may not be justly required of the Roman Catholics? And whether, in common prudence or policy, any priest should be tolerated who refuseth to take it?

291. Qu. Whether there have not been Popish recusants? and, if so, whether it would be right to object against the foregoing oath, that all would take it, and none think themselves bound by it?

292. Qu. Whether those of the Church of Rome, in converting the Moors of Spain or the Protestants of France, have not set us an example which might justify a similar treatment of themselves, if the laws of Christianity allowed thereof?

293. Qu. Whether compelling men to a profession of faith is not the worst thing in Popery, and, consequently, whether to copy after the Church of Rome therein, were not to become Papists ourselves in the worst sense?

294. Qu. Whether, nevertheless, we may not imitate the Church of Rome, in certain places, where Jews are tolerated, by obliging our Irish Papists, at stated times, to hear Protestant sermons? and whether this would not make missionaries in the Irish tongue useful?

295. Qu. Whether the mere act of hearing, without making any profession of faith, or joining in any part of worship, be a religious act; and, consequently, whether their being obliged to hear, may not consist with the toleration of Roman Catholics?

296. Qu. Whether, if penal laws should be thought oppressive, we may not at least be allowed to give premiums? And whether it would be wrong, if the public encouraged Popish families to become hearers, by paying their hearth-money for them?

297. Qu. Whether in granting toleration, we ought not to distinguish between doctrines purely religious, and such as affect the State?

298. Qu. Whether the case be not very different in regard to a man who only eats fish on Fridays, says his prayers in Latin, or believes transubstantiation, and one who professeth in temporals a subjection to foreign powers, who holdeth himself absolved from all obedience to his natural prince and the laws of his country?

who is even persuaded, it may be meritorious to destroy the powers that are?

299. Qu. Whether, therefore, a distinction should not be made between mere Papists and recusants? And whether the latter can expect the same protection from the Government as the former?

300. Qu. Whether our Papists in this kingdom can complain, if they are allowed to be as much Papists as the subjects of France or of the Empire?

301. Qu. Whether there is any such thing as a body of inhabitants, in any Roman Catholic country under the sun, that profess an absolute submission to the pope's orders in matters of an indifferent nature, or that in such points do not think it their duty to obey the civil government?

302. Qu. Whether since the peace of Utrecht, mass was not celebrated and the sacraments administered in divers dioceses of Sicily, notwithstanding the Pope's interdict?

303. Qu. Whether every plea of conscience is to be regarded? Whether, for instance, the German Anabaptists, Levellers, or Fifth Monarchy men would be tolerated on that pretence?

304. Qu. Whether Popish children bred in charity schools, when bound out in apprenticeship to Protestant masters, do generally continue Protestants?

305. Qu. Whether a Sum, which would go but a little way towards erecting hospitals for maintaining and educating the children of the native Irish, might not go far in binding them out apprentices to Protestant masters, for husbandry, useful trades, and the service of families?

306. Qu. Whether if the parents are overlooked, there can be any great hopes of success in converting the children?

307. Qu. Whether there be any instance, of a people's being converted in a Christian sense, otherwise than by preaching to them and instructing them in their own language?

308. Qu. Whether catechists in the Irish tongue may not easily be procured and subsisted? And whether this would not be the most practicable means for converting the natives?

309. Qu. Whether it be not of great advantage to the Church of Rome, that she hath clergy suited to all ranks of men, in gradual subordination from cardinals down to mendicants?

310. Qu. Whether her numerous poor clergy are not very useful in missions, and of much influence with the people?

311. Qu. Whether, in defect of able missionaries, persons conversant in low life, and speaking the Irish tongue, if well instructed in the first principles of religion, and in the popish controversy, though for the rest on a level with the parish clerks, or the school-masters of charity-schools, may not be fit to mix with and bring over our poor illiterate natives to the Established Church? Whether it is not to be wished that some parts of our liturgy and homilies were publicly read in the Irish language? And whether, in these views, it may not be right to breed up some of the better sort of children in the charity-schools, and qualify them for missionaries, catechists, and readers?

312. Qu. Whether there be any nation of men governed by reason? And yet, if there was not, whether this would be a good argument against the use of reason in pubic affairs?

313. Qu. Whether, as others have supposed an Atlantis or Utopia, we also may not suppose an Hyperborean island inhabited by reasonable creatures?

314. Qu. Whether an indifferent person, who looks into all hands, may not be a better judge of the game than a party who sees only his own?

315. Qu. Whether one, whose end is to make his countrymen think, may not gain his end, even though they should not think as he doth?

316. Qu. Whether he, who only asks, asserts? and whether any man can fairly confute the querist?

317. Qu. Whether the interest of a part will not always be preferred to that of the whole?

Part II

Query I.

Whether there be any country in Christendom more capable of improvement than Ireland?

2. Qu. Whether we are not as far before other nations with respect to natural advantages, as we are behind them with respect to arts and industry?

3. Qu. Whether we do not live in a most fertile soil and temperate climate, and yet whether our people in general do not feel great want and misery?

4. Qu. Whether my countrymen are not readier at finding excuses than remedies?

5. Qu. Whether it can be reasonably hoped, that our state will mend, so long as property is insecure among us?

6. Qu. Whether in that case the wisest government, or the best laws can avail. us?

7. Qu. Whether a few mishaps to particular persons may not throw this nation into the utmost confusion?

8. Qu. Whether the public is not even on the brink of being undone by private accidents?

9. Qu. Whether the wealth and prosperity of our country do not hang by a hair, the probity of one banker, the caution of another, and the lives of all?

10. Qu. Whether we have not been sufficiently admonished of this by some late events?

11. Qu. Whether therefore it be not high time to open our eyes?

12. Qu. Whether a national bank would not at once secure our properties, put an end to usury, facilitate commerce, supply the want of coin, and produce ready payments in all parts of the kingdom?

13. Qu. Whether the use or nature of money, which all men so eagerly pursue, be yet sufficiently understood or considered by all?

14. Qu. Whether mankind are not governed by Citation rather than by reason?

15. Qu. Whether there be not a measure or limit, within which gold and silver are useful, and beyond which they may be hurtful?

16. Qu. Whether that measure be not the circulating of industry?

17. Qu. Whether a discovery of the richest gold mine that ever was, in the heart of this kingdom, would be a real advantage to us?

18. Qu. Whether it would not tempt foreigners to prey upon us?

19. Qu. Whether it would not render us a lazy, proud, and dastardly people?

20. Qu. Whether every man who had money enough would not be a gentleman? And whether a nation of gentlemen would not be a wretched nation?

21. Qu. Whether all things would not bear a high price? And whether men would not increase their fortunes without being the better for it?

22. Qu. Whether the same evils would be apprehended from paper-money under an honest and thrifty regulation?

23. Qu. Whether, therefore, a national bank would not be more beneficial than even a mine of gold?

24. Qu. Whether private ends are not prosecuted with more attention and vigour than the public? And yet, whether all private ends are not included in the pubic?

25. Qu. Whether banking be not absolutely necessary to the pubic weal?

26. Qu. Whether even our private banks, though attended with such hazards as we all know them to be, are not of singular use in defect of a national bank?

27. Qu. Whether without them what little business and industry there is would not stagnate? But whether it be not a mighty privilege for a private person to be able to create a hundred pounds with a dash of his pen?

28. Qu. Whether the mystery of banking did not derive its original from the Italians? Whether this acute people were not, upon a time, bankers over all Europe? Whether that business was not practised by some of their noblest families who made immense profits by it, and whether to that the house of Medici did not originally owe its greatness?

29. Qu. Whether the wise state of Venice was not the first that conceived the advantage of a national bank?

30. Qu. Whether at Venice all payments of bills of exchange and merchants' contracts are not made in the national or pubic bank, the greatest affairs being transacted only by writing the names of the parties, one as debtor the other as creditor in the bank-book?

31. Qu. Whether nevertheless it was not found expedient to provide a chest of ready cash for answering all demands that should happen to be made on account of payments in detail?

32. Qu. Whether this offer of ready cash, instead of transfers in the bank, hath not been found to augment rather than diminish the stock thereof?

33. Qu. Whether at Venice, the difference in the value of bank money above other money be not fixed at twenty per cent?

34. Qu. Whether the bank of Venice be not shut up four times in the year twenty days each time?

35. Qu. Whether by means of this bank the public be not mistress of a million and a half sterling?

36. Qu. Whether the great exactness and integrity with which this bank is managed be not the chief support of that republic?

37. Qu. Whether we may not hope for as much skill and honesty in a Protestant Irish Parliament as in a Popish Senate of Venice?

38. Qu. Whether the bank of Amsterdam was not begun about one hundred and thirty years ago, and whether at this day its stock be not conceived to amount to three thousand tons of gold, or thirty millions sterling?

39. Qu. Whether besides coined money, there be not also great quantities of ingots or bars of gold and silver lodged in this bank?

40. Qu. Whether all payments of contracts for goods in gross, and letters of exchange, must not be made by transfers in the bank-books, provided the sum exceed three hundred florins?

41. Qu. Whether it be not true, that the bank of Amsterdam never makes payments in cash?

42. Qu. Whether, nevertheless, it be not also true, that no man who hath credit in the bank can want money from particular persons, who are willing to become creditors in his stead?

43. Qu. Whether any man thinks himself the poorer, because his money is in the bank?

44. Qu. Whether the creditors of the bank of Amsterdam are not at liberty to withdraw their money when they please, and whether this liberty doth not make them less desirous to use it?

45. Qu. Whether this bank be not shut up twice in the year for ten or fifteen days, during which time the accounts are balanced?

46. Qu. Whether it be not owing to this bank that the city of Amsterdam, without the least confusion, hazard, or trouble, maintains and every day promotes so general and quick a circulation of industry?

47. Qu. Whether it be not the greatest help and spur to commerce that property can be so readily conveyed and so well secured by a compte en banc, that is, by only writing one man's name for another's in the bank-book?

48. Qu. Whether, at the beginning of the last century, those who had lent money to the public during the war with Spain were not satisfied by the sole expedient of placing their names in a compte en banc, with liberty to transfer their claims?

49. Qu. Whether the example of those easy transfers in the compte en banc, thus casually erected, did not tempt other men to become creditors to the public, in order to profit by the same

secure and expeditious method of keeping and transferring their wealth?

50. Qu. Whether this compte en banc hath not proved better than a mine of gold to Amsterdam?

51. Qu. Whether that city may not be said to owe her greatness to the unpromising accident of her having been in debt more than she was able to Pay?

52. Qu. Whether it be known that any State from such small beginnings, in so short a time, ever grew to so great wealth and power as the province of Holland hath done; and whether the bank of Amsterdam hath not been the real cause of such extraordinary growth?

53. Qu. Whether we are by nature a more stupid people than the Dutch? And yet whether these things are sufficiently considered by our patriots?

54. Qu. Whether anything less than the utter subversion of those Republics can break the banks of Venice and Amsterdam?

55. Qu. Whether at Hamburgh the citizens have not the management of the bank, without the meddling or inspection of the Senate?

56. Qu. Whether the directors be not four principal burghers chosen by plurality of voices, whose business is to see the rules observed, and furnish the cashiers with money?

57. Qu. Whether the book-keepers are not obliged to balance their accounts every week, and exhibit them to the controllers or directors?

58. Qu. Whether any besides the citizens are admitted to have compte en banc at Hamburgh?

59. Qu. Whether there be not a certain limit, under which no sum can be entered into the bank?

60. Qu. Whether each particular person doth not pay a fee in order to be admitted to a compte en banc at Hamburgh and Amsterdam?

61. Qu. Whether the effects lodged in the bank of Hamburgh are liable to be seized for debt or forfeiture?

62. Qu. Whether this bank doth not lend money upon pawns at low interest and only for half a year, after which term, in default of payment, the pawns are punctually sold by auction?

63. Qu. Whether the book-keepers of the bank of Hamburgh are not obliged upon oath never to reveal what sums of money are paid in or out of the bank, or what effects any particular person has therein?

64. Qu. Whether, therefore, it be possible to know the state or stock of this bank; and yet whether it be not of the greatest reputation and most established credit throughout the North?

65. Qu. Whether the success of those public banks in Venice, Amsterdam and Hamburg would not naturally produce in other States an inclination to the same methods?

66. Qu. Whether an absolute monarchy be so apt to gain credit, and whether the vivacity of some humours could so well suit with the slow steps and discreet management which a bank requires?

67. Qu. Whether the bank called the general bank of France, contrived by Mr Law, and established by letters patent in May,

1716, was not in truth a particular and not a national bank, being in the hands of a particular company privileged and protected by the Government?

68. Qu. Whether the Government did not order that the notes of this bank should pass on a par with ready money in all payments of the revenue?

69. Qu. Whether this bank was not obliged to issue only such notes as were payable at sight?

70. Qu. Whether it was not made a capital crime to forge the notes of this bank?

71. Qu. Whether this bank was not restrained from trading either by sea or land, and from taking up money upon interest?

72. Qu. Whether the original stock thereof was not six millions of livres, divided into actions of a thousand crowns each?

73. Qu. Whether the proprietors were not to hold general assemblies twice in the year, for the regulating of their affairs?

74. Qu. Whether the accompts of this bank were not balanced twice every year?

75. Qu. Whether there were not two chests belonging to this bank, the one called the general chest containing their specie, their bills and their copper plates for the printing of those bills, under the custody of three locks, whereof the keys were kept by the director, the inspector and treasurer. also another called, the ordinary chest, containing part of the stock not exceeding two hundred thousand crowns, under the key of the treasurer?

76. Qu. Whether out of this last mentioned sum, each particular cashier was not to be intrusted with a share not exceeding the

value of twenty thousand crowns at a time, and that under good security?

77. Qu. Whether the Regent did not reserve to himself the power of calling this bank to account, so often as he should think good, and of appointing the inspector?

78. Qu. Whether in the beginning of the year 1719 the French King did not convert the general bank of France into a Banque Royale, having himself purchased the stock of the company and taken it into his own hands, and appointed the Duke of Orleans chief manager thereof?

79. Qu. Whether from that time, all matters relating to the bank were not transacted in the name, and by the sole authority, of the king?

80. Qu. Whether his Majesty did not undertake to receive and keep the cash of all particular persons, subjects, or foreigners, in his said Royale Banque, without being paid for that trouble? And whether it was not declared, that such cash should not be liable to seizure on any pretext, not even on the king's own account?

81. Qu. Whether the treasurer alone did not sign all the bills, receive all the stock paid into the bank, and keep account of all the ingoings and out-goings?

82. Qu. Whether there were not three registers for the enregistering of the bills kept in the Banque Royale, one by the inspector, another by the controller, and a third by the treasurer?

83. Qu. Whether there was not also a fourth register, containing the profits of the bank, which was visited, at least once a week, by the inspector and controller?

84. Qu. Whether, beside the general bureau or compter in the city of Paris, there were not also appointed five more in the towns of Lyons, Tours, Rochelle, Orleans, and Amiens, each whereof was provided with two chests, one of specie for discharging bills at sight, and another of bank bills to be issued as there should be demand?

85. Qu. Whether, in the above mentioned towns, it was not prohibited to make payments in silver, exceeding the sum of six hundred livres?

86. Qu. Whether all creditors were not empowered to demand payment in bank bills instead of specie?

87. Qu. Whether, in a short compass of time, this bank did not undergo many new changes and regulations by several successive acts of council?

88. Qu. Whether the untimely, repeated, and boundless fabrication of bills did not precipitate the ruin of this bank?

89. Qu. Whether it be not true, that before the end of July, 1719, they had fabricated four hundred millions of livres in bank-notes, to which they added the sum of one hundred and twenty millions more on the twelfth of September following, also the same sum of one hundred and twenty millions on the twenty-fourth of 3 October, and again on the twenty-ninth of December, in the same year, the farther sum of three hundred and sixty millions, making the whole, from an original stock of six millions, mount, within the compass of one year, to a thousand millions of livres?

90. Qu. Whether on the twenty-eighth of February, 1720, the king did not make an union of the bank with the united company of the East and West Indies, which from that time had the administration and profits of the Banque Royale?

91. Qu. Whether the king did not still profess himself responsible for the value of the bank bills, and whether the company were not responsible to his Majesty for their management?

92. Qu. Whether sixteen hundred millions of livres, lent to his majesty by the company, was not a sufficient pledge to indemnify the king?

93. Qu. Whether the new directors were not prohibited to make any more bills without an act of council?

94. Qu. Whether the chests and books of the Banque were not subjected to the joint inspection of a Counsellor of State, and the Prevot des Marchands, assisted by two Echevins, a judge, and a consul, who had power to visit when they would and without warning?

95. Qu. Whether in less than two years the actions or shares of the Indian Company (first established for Mississippi, and afterwards increased by the addition of other compares and further? and whether this privileges) did not rise to near 2000 per cent must be ascribed to real advantages of trade, or to mere frenzy?

96. Qu. Whether, from first to last, there were not fabricated bank bills, of one kind or other, to the value of more than two thousand and six hundred millions of livres, or one hundred and thirty millions sterling?

97. Qu. Whether the credit of the bank did not decline from its union with the Indian Company?

98. Qu. Whether, notwithstanding all the above-mentioned extraordinary measures, the bank bills did not still pass at par with gold and silver to May, 1720, when the French king thought

fit, by a new act of council, to make a reduction of their value, which proved a fatal blow, the effects whereof, though soon retracted, no subsequent skill or management could ever repair?

99. Qu. Whether, what no reason, reflexion, or foresight could do, this simple matter of fact (the most powerful argument with the multitude) did not do at once, to wit, open the eyes of the people?

100. Qu. Whether the dealers in that sort of ware had ever troubled their heads with the nature of credit, or the true use and end of banks, but only considered their bills and actions as things, to which the general demand gave a price?

101. Qu. Whether the Government was not in great perplexity to contrive expedients for the getting rid of those bank bills, which had been lately multiplied with such an unlimited passion?

102. Qu. Whether notes to the value of about ninety millions were not sunk by being paid off in specie, with the cash of the Compagnie des Indes, with that of the bank, and that of the Hotels des Monnoyes? Whether five hundred and thirty millions were not converted into annuities at the royal treasury? Whether several hundred millions more in bank bills were not extinguished and replaced by annuities on the City of Paris, on taxes throughout the provinces, &c., &c?

103. Qu. Whether, after all other shifts, the last and grand resource for exhausting that ocean, was not the erecting of a compte en banc in several towns of France?

104. Qu. Whether, when the imagination of a people is thoroughly wrought upon and heated by their own example, and the arts of designing men, this doth not produce a sort of enthusiasm which takes place of reason, and is the most dangerous distemper in a State?

105. Qu. Whether this epidemical madness should not be always before the eyes of a legislature, in the framing of a national bank?

106. Qu. Whether, therefore, it may not be fatal to engraft trade on a national bank, or to propose dividends on the stock thereof?

107. Qu. Whether it be possible for a national bank to subsist and maintain its credit under a French government?

108. Qu. Whether it may not be as useful a lesson to consider the bad management of some as the good management of others?

109. Qu. Whether the rapid and surprising success of the schemes of those who directed the French bank did not turn their brains?

110. Qu. Whether the best institutions may not be made subservient to bad ends?

111. Qu. Whether, as the aim of industry is power, and the aim of a bank is to circulate and secure this power to each individual, it doth not follow that absolute power in one hand is inconsistent with a lasting and a flourishing bank?

112. Qu. Whether our natural appetites, as well as powers, are not limited to their respective ends and uses? But whether artificial appetites may not be infinite?

113. Qu. Whether the simple getting of money, or passing it from hand to hand without industry, be an object worthy of a wise government?

114. Qu. Whether, if money be considered as an end, the appetite thereof be not infinite? But whether the ends of money itself be not bounded?

115. Qu. Whether the mistaking of the means for the end was not a fundamental error in the French councils?

116. Qu. Whether the total sum of all other powers, be it of enjoyment or action, which belong to man, or to all mankind together, is not in truth a very narrow and limited quantity? But whether fancy is not boundless?

117. Qu. Whether this capricious tyrant, which usurps the place of reason, doth not most cruelly torment and delude those poor men, the usurers, stockjobbers, and projectors, of content to themselves from heaping up riches, that is, from gathering counters, from multiplying figures, from enlarging denominations, without knowing what they would be at, and without having a proper regard to the use or end or nature of things?

118. Qu. Whether the ignis fatuus of fancy doth not kindle immoderate desires, and lead men into endless pursuits and wild labyrinths?

119. Qu. Whether counters be not referred to other things, which, so long as they keep pace and proportion with the counters, it must be owned the counters are useful; but whether beyond that to value or covet counters be not direct folly?

120. Qu. Whether the public aim ought not to be, that men's industry should supply their present wants, and the overplus be converted into a stock of power?

121. Qu. Whether the better this power is secured, and the more easily it is transferred, industry be not so much the more encouraged?

122. Qu. Whether money, more than is expedient for those purposes, be not upon the whole hurtful rather than beneficial to a State?

123. Qu. Whether there should not be a constant care to keep the bills at par?

124. Qu. Whether, therefore, bank bills should at any time be multiplied but as trade and business were also multiplied?

125. Qu. Whether it was not madness in France to mint bills and actions, merely to humour the people and rob them of their cash?

126. Qu. Whether we may not profit by their mistakes, and as some things are to be avoided, whether there may not be others worthy of imitation in the conduct of our neighbours?

127. Qu. Whether the way be not clear and open and easy, and whether anything but the will is wanting to our legislature?

128. Qu. Whether jobs and tricks are not detested on all hands, but whether it be not the joint interest of prince and people to promote industry?

129. Qu. Whether, all things considered, a national bank be not the most practicable, sure, and speedy method to mend our affairs, and cause industry to flourish among us?

130. Qu. Whether a compte en banc or current bank bills would best answer our occasions?

131. Qu. Whether a public compte en banc, where effects are received, and accounts kept with particular persons, be not an excellent expedient for a great city?

132. Qu. What effect a general compte en banc would have in the metropolis of this kingdom with one in each province subordinate thereunto?

133. Qu. Whether it may not be proper for a great kingdom to unite both expedients, to wit, bank notes and a compte en banc?

134. Qu. Whether, nevertheless, it would be advisable to begin with both at once, or rather to proceed first with the bills, and afterwards, as business multiplied, and money or effects flowed in, to open the compte en banc?

135. Qu. Whether, for greater security, double books of compte en banc should not be kept in different places and hands?

136. Qu. Whether it would not be right to build the compters and public treasuries, where books and bank notes are kept, without wood, all arched and floored with brick or stone, having chests also and cabinets of iron?

137. Qu. Whether divers registers of the bank notes should not be kept in different hands?

138. Qu. Whether there should not be great discretion in the uttering of bank notes, and whether the attempting to do things per saltum be not often the way to undo them?

139. Qu. Whether the main art be not by slow degrees and cautious measures to reconcile the bank to the public, to wind it insensibly into the affections of men, and interweave it with the constitution?

140. Qu. Whether the promoting of industry should not be always in view, as the true and sole end, the rule and measure, of a national bank? And whether all deviations from that object should not be carefully avoided?

141. Qu. Whether a national bank may not prevent the drawing of specie out of the country (where it circulates in small payments), to be shut up in the chests of particular persons?

142. Qu. Whether it may not be useful, for supplying manufactures and trade with stock, for regulating exchange, for quickening commerce, for putting spirit into the people?

143. Qu. Whether tenants or debtors could have cause to complain of our monies being reduced to the English value if it were withal multiplied in the same, or in a greater proportion? and whether this would not be the consequence of a national bank?

144. Qu. If there be an open sure way to thrive, without hazard to ourselves or prejudice to our neighbours, what should hinder us from putting it in practice?

145. Qu. Whether in so numerous a Senate, as that of this kingdom, it may not be easie to find men of pure hands and clear heads fit to contrive and model a public bank?

146. Qu. Whether a view of the precipice be not sufficient, or whether we must tumble headlong before we are roused?

147. Qu. Whether in this drooping and dispirited country, men are quite awake?

148. Qu. Whether we are sufficiently sensible of the peculiar security there is in having a bank that consists of land and paper, one of which cannot be exported, and the other is in no danger of being exported?

149. Qu. Whether it be not delightful to complain? And whether there be not many who had rather utter their complaints than redress their evils?

150. Qu. Whether, if 'the crown of the wise be their riches' (Prov., xiv.24), we are not the foolishest people in Christendom?

151. Qu. Whether we have not all the while great civil as well as natural advantages?

152. Qu. Whether there be any people who have more leisure to cultivate the arts of peace, and study the public weal?

153. Qu. Whether other nations who enjoy any share of freedom, and have great objects in view, be not unavoidably embarrassed and distracted by factions? But whether we do not divide upon trifles, and whether our parties are not a burlesque upon politics?

154. Qu. Whether it be not an advantage that we are not embroiled in foreign affairs, that we hold not the balance of Europe, that we are protected by other fleets and armies, that it is the true interest of a powerful people, from whom we are descended, to guard us on all sides?

155. Qu. Whether England doth not really love us and wish well to us, as bone of her bone, and flesh of her flesh? And whether it be not our part to cultivate this love and affection all manner of ways?

156. Qu. Whether, if we do not reap the benefits that may be made of our country and government, want of will in the lower people, or want of wit in the upper, be most in fault?

157. Qu. What sea-ports or foreign trade have the Swisses; and yet how warm are those people, and how well provided?

158. Qu. Whether there may not be found a people who so contrive as to be impoverished by their trade? And whether we are not that people?

159. Qu. Whether it would not be better for this island, if all our fine folk of both sexes were shipped off, to remain in foreign countries, rather than that they should spend their estates at home

in foreign luxury, and spread the contagion thereof through their native land?

160. Qu. Whether our gentry understand or have a notion of magnificence, and whether for want thereof they do not affect very wretched distinctions?

161. Qu. Whether there be not an art or skill in governing human pride, so as to render it subservient to the pubic aim?

162. Qu. Whether the great and general aim of the public should not be to employ the people?

163. Qu. What right an eldest son hath to the worst education?

164. Qu. Whether men's counsels are not the result of their knowledge and their principles?

165. Qu. Whether an assembly of freethinkers, petit maitres, and smart Fellows would not make an admirable Senate?

166. Qu. Whether there be not labour of the brains as well as of the hands, and whether the former is beneath a gentleman?

167. Qu. Whether the public be more interested to protect the property acquired by mere birth than that which is the Mediate fruit of learning and vertue?

168. Qu. Whether it would not be a poor and ill-judged project to attempt to promote the good of the community, by invading the rights of one part thereof, or of one particular order of men?

169. Qu. Whether the public happiness be not proposed by the legislature, and whether such happiness doth not contain that of the individuals?

170. Qu. Whether, therefore, a legislator should be content with a vulgar share of knowledge? Whether he should not be a person of reflexion and thought, who hath made it his study to understand the true nature and interest of mankind, how to guide men's humours and passions, how to incite their active powers, how to make their several talents co-operate to the mutual benefit of each other, and the general good of the whole?

171. Qu. Whether it doth not follow that above all things a gentleman's care should be to keep his own faculties sound and entire?

172. Qu. Whether the natural phlegm of this island needs any additional stupefier?

173. Qu. Whether all spirituous liquors are not in truth opiates?

174. Qu. Whether our men of business are not generally very grave by fifty?

175. Qu. Whether there be really among us any parents so silly, as to encourage drinking in their children?

176. Qu. Whence it is, that our ladies are more alive, and bear age so much better than our gentlemen?

177. Qu. Whether all men have not faculties of mind or body which may be employed for the public benefit?

178. Qu. Whether the main point be not to multiply and employ our people?

179. Qu. Whether hearty food and warm clothing would not enable and encourage the lower sort to labour?

180. Qu. Whether, in such a soil as ours, if there was industry, there could be want?

181. Qu. Whether the way to make men industrious be not to let them taste the fruits of their industry? And whether the labouring ox should be muzzled?

182. Qu. Whether our landlords are to be told that industry and numbers would raise the value of their lands, or that one acre about the Tholsel is worth ten thousand acres in Connaught?

183. Qu. Whether our old native Irish are not the most indolent and supine people in Christendom?

184. Qu. Whether they are yet civilized, and whether their habitations and furniture are not more sordid than those of the savage Americans?

185. Qu. Whether this be altogether their own fault?

186. Qu. Whether it be not a sad circumstance to live among lazy beggars? And whether, on the other hand, it would not be delightful to live in a country swarming, like China, with busy people?

187. Qu. Whether we should not cast about, by all manner of means, to excite industry, and to remove whatever hinders it? And whether every one should not lend a helping hand?

188. Qu. Whether vanity itself should not be engaged in this good work? And whether it is not to be wished that the finding of employment for themselves and others were a fashionable distinction among the ladies?

189. Qu. Whether idleness be the mother or the daughter of spleen?

190. Qu. Whether it may not be worth while to publish the conversation of Ischomachus and his wife in Xenophon, for the use of our ladies?

191. Qu. Whether it is true that there have been, upon a time, one hundred millions of people employed in China, without the woollen trade, or any foreign commerce?

192. Qu. Whether the natural inducements to sloth are not greater in the Mogul's country than in Ireland, and yet whether, in that suffocating and dispiriting climate, the Banyans are not all, men, women, and children, constantly employed?

193. Qu. Whether it be not true that the great Mogul's subjects might undersell us even in our own markets, and clothe our people with their stuffs and calicoes, if they were imported duty free?

194. Qu. Whether there can be a greater reproach on the leading men and the patriots of a country, than that the people should want employment? And whether methods may not be found to employ even the lame and the blind, the dumb, the deaf, and the maimed, in some or other branch of our manufactures?

195. Qu. Whether much may not be expected from a biennial consultation of so many wise men about the public good?

196. Qu. Whether a tax upon dirt would not be one way of encouraging industry?

197. Qu. Whether it may not be right to appoint censors in every parish to observe and make returns of the idle hands?

198. Qu. Whether a register or history of the idleness and industry of a people would be an useless thing?

199. Qu. Whether we are apprized, of all the uses that may be made of political arithmetic?

200. Qu. Whether it would be a great hardship if every parish were obliged to find work for their poor?

201. Qu. Whether children especially should not be inured to labour betimes?

202. Qu. Whether there should not be erected, in each province, an hospital for orphans and foundlings, at the expense of old bachelors?

203. Qu. Whether it be true that in the Dutch workhouses things are so managed that a child four years old may earn its own livelihood?

204. Qu. What a folly is it to build fine houses, or establish lucrative posts and large incomes, under the notion of providing for the poor?

205. Qu. Whether the poor, grown up and in health, need any other provision but their own industry, under public inspection?

206. Qu. Whether the poor-tax in England hath lessened or increased the number of the poor?

207. Qu. Why the workhouse in Dublin, with so good an endowment, should yet be of so little use? and whether this may not be owing to that very endowment?

208. Qu. Whether that income might not, by this time, have gone through the whole kingdom, and erected a dozen workhouses in every county?

209. Qu. Whether workhouses should not be made at the least expense, with clay floors, and walls of rough stone, without plastering, ceiling, or glazing?

210. Qu. Whether the tax on chairs or hackney coaches be not paid, rather by the country gentlemen, than the citizens of Dublin?

211. Qu. Whether it be an impossible attempt to set our people at work, or whether industry be a habit which, like other habits, may by time and skill be introduced among any people?

212. Qu. Whether all manner of means should not be employed to possess the nation in general with an aversion and contempt for idleness and all idle folk?

213. Qu. Whether it would be a hardship on people destitute of all things, if the public furnished them with necessaries which they should be obliged to earn by their labour?

214. Qu. Whether other nations have not found great benefit from the use of slaves in repairing high roads, making rivers navigable, draining bogs, erecting public buildings, bridges, and manufactures?

215. Qu. Whether temporary servitude would not be the best cure for idleness and beggary?

216. Qu. Whether the public hath not a right to employ those who cannot or who will not find employment for themselves?

217. Qu. Whether all sturdy beggars should not be seized and made slaves to the public for a certain term of years?

218. Qu. Whether he who is chained in a jail or dungeon hath not, for the time, lost his liberty? And if so, whether temporary slavery be not already admitted among us?

219. Qu. Whether a state of servitude, wherein he should be well worked, fed, and clothed, would not be a preferment to such a fellow?

220. Qu. Whether criminals in the freest country may not forfeit their liberty, and repair the damage they have done the public by hard labour?

221. Qu. What the word 'servant' signifies in the New Testament?

222. Qu. Whether the view of criminals chained in pairs and kept at hard labour would not be very edifying to the multitude?

223. Qu. Whether the want of such an institution be not plainly seen in England, where the disbelief of a future state hardeneth rogues against the fear of death, and where, through the great growth of robbers and housebreakers, it becomes every day more necessary?

224. Qu. Whether it be not easier to prevent than to remedy, and whether we should not profit by the example of others?

225. Qu. Whether felons are not often spared, and therefore encouraged, by the compassion of those who should prosecute them?

226. Qu. Whether many that would not take away the life of a thief may not nevertheless be willing to bring him to a more adequate punishment?

227. Qu. Whether there should not be a difference between the treatment of criminals and that of other slaves?

228. Qu. Whether the most indolent would be fond of idleness, if they regarded it as the sure road to hard labour?

229. Qu. Whether the industry of the lower part of our people doth not much depend on the expense of the upper?

230. Qu. What would be the consequence if our gentry affected to distinguish themselves by fine houses rather than fine clothes?

231. Qu. Whether any people in Europe are so meanly provided with houses and furniture, in proportion to their incomes, as the men of estates in Ireland?

232. Qu. Whether building would not peculiarly encourage all other arts in this kingdom?

233. Qu. Whether smiths, masons, bricklayers, plasterers, carpenters, joiners, tilers, plumbers, and glaziers would not all find employment if the humour of building prevailed?

234. Qu. Whether the ornaments and furniture of a good house do not employ a number of all sorts of artificers, in iron, wood, marble, brass, pewter, copper, wool, flax, and divers other materials?

235. Qu. Whether in buildings and gardens a great number of day-labourers do not find employment?

236. Qu. Whether by these means much of that sustenance and wealth of this nation which now goes to foreigners would not be kept at home, and nourish and circulate among our own people?

237. Qu. Whether, as industry produced good living, the number of hands and mouths would not be increased; and in proportion thereunto, whether there would not be every day more occasion for agriculture? And whether this article alone would not employ a world of people?

238. Qu. Whether such management would not equally provide for the magnificence of the rich, and the necessities of the poor?

239. Qu. Whether an expense in building and improvements doth not remain at home, pass to the heir, and adorn the public? And whether any of those things can be said of claret?

240. Qu. Whether fools do not make fashions, and wise men follow them?

241. Qu. Whether, for one who hurts his fortune by improvements, twenty do not ruin themselves by foreign luxury?

242. Qu. Whether in proportion as Ireland was improved and beautified by fine seats, the number of absentees would not decrease?

243. Qu. Whether he who employs men in buildings and manufactures doth not put life in the country, and whether the neighbourhood round him be not observed to thrive?

244. Qu. Whether money circulated on the landlord's own lands, and among his own tenants, doth not return into his own pocket?

245. Qu. Whether every squire that made his domain swarm with busy hands, like a bee-hive or ant-hill, would not serve his own interest, as well as that of his country?

246. Qu. Whether a gentleman who hath seen a little of the world, and observed how men live elsewhere, can contentedly sit

down in a cold, damp, sordid habitation, in the midst of a bleak country, inhabited by thieves and beggars?

247. Qu. Whether, on the other hand, a handsome seat amidst well-improved lands, fair villages, and a thriving neighbourhood may not invite a man to dwell on his own estate, and quit the life of an insignificant saunterer about town for that of a useful country-gentleman?

248. Qu. Whether it would not be of use and ornament if the towns throughout this kingdom were provided with decent churches, townhouses, workhouses, market-places, and paved streets, with some order taken for cleanliness?

249. Qu. Whether, if each of these towns were addicted to some peculiar manufacture, we should not find that the employing many hands together on the same work was the way to perfect our workmen? And whether all these things might not soon be provided by a domestic industry, if money were not wanting?

250. Qu. Whether money could ever be wanting to the demands of industry, if we had a national bank?

251. Qu. Whether when a motion was made once upon a time to establish a private bank in this kingdom by public authority, divers gentlemen did not shew themselves forward to embark in that design?

252. Qu. Whether it may not now be hoped, that our patriots will be as forward to examine and consider the proposal of a public bank calculated only for the public good?

253. Qu. Whether any people upon earth shew a more early zeal for the service of their country, greater eagerness to bear a part in the legislature, or a more general parturiency with respect to politics and public counsels?

254. Qu. Whether, nevertheless, a light and ludicrous vein be not the reigning humour; but whether there was ever greater cause to be serious?

Part III

Query I.

Whether the fable of Hercules and the carter ever suited any nation like this nation of Ireland?

2. Qu. Whether it be not a new spectacle under the sun, to behold, in such a climate and such a soil, and under such a gentle government, so many roads untrodden, fields untilled, houses desolate, and hands unemployed?

3. Qu. Whether there is any country in Christendom, either kingdom or republic, depending or independent, free or enslaved, which may not afford us a useful lesson?

4. Qu. Whether the frugal Swisses have any other commodities but their butter and cheese and a few cattle, for exportation; whether, nevertheless, the single canton of Berne hath not in her public treasury two millions sterling?

5. Qu. Whether that small town of Berne, with its scanty barren territory, in a mountainous corner, without sea-ports, without manufactures, without mines, be not rich by mere dint of frugality?

6. Qu. Whether the Swisses in general have not sumptuary laws, prohibiting the use of gold, jewels, silver, silk, and lace in their apparel, and indulging the women only to wear silk on festivals, weddings, and public solemnities?

7. Qu. Whether there be not two ways of growing rich, sparing and getting? But whether the lazy spendthrift must not be doubly poor?

8. Qu. Whether money circulating be not the life of industry; and whether the want thereof doth not render a State gouty and inactive?

9. Qu. But whether, if we had a national bank, and our present cash (small as it is) were put into the most convenient shape, men should hear any public complaints for want of money?

10. Qu. Whether all circulation be not alike a circulation of credit, whatsoever medium (metal or paper) is employed, and whether gold be any more than credit for so much power?

11. Qu. Whether the wealth of the richest nations in Christendom doth not consist in paper vastly more than in gold and silver?

12. Qu. Whether Lord Clarendon doth not aver of his own knowledge, that the Prince of Orange, with the best credit, and the assistance of the richest men in Amsterdam, was above ten days endeavouring to raise L20,000 in specie, without being able to raise half the sum in all that time? (See Clarendon's History, BK. XII)

13. Qu. Whether the whole city of Amsterdam would not have been troubled to have brought together twenty thousand pounds in one room?

14. Qu. Whether it be not absolutely necessary that there must be a bank and must be a trust? And, if so, whether it be not the most safe and prudent course to have a national bank and trust the legislature?

15. Qu. Whether objections against trust in general avail, when it is allowed there must be a trust, and the only question is where to place this trust, whether in the legislature or in private hands?

16. Qu. Whether it can be expected that private persons should have more regard to the public than the public itself?

17. Qu. Whether, if there be hazards from mismanagement, those may not be provided against in the framing of a pubic bank; but whether any provision can be made against the mismanagement of private banks that are under no check, control, or inspection?

18. Qu. Whatever may be said for the sake of objecting, yet, whether it be not false in fact, that men would prefer a private security to a public security?

19. Qu. Whether a national bank ought to be considered as a new experiment; and whether it be not a motive to try this scheme that it hath been already tried with success in other countries?

20. Qu. If power followeth money, whether this can be anywhere more properly and securely placed, than in the same hands wherein the supreme power is already placed?

21. Qu. Whether there be more danger of abuse in a private than in a public management?

22. Qu. Whether the proper usual remedy for abuses of private banks be not to bring them before Parliament, and subject them to the inspection of a committee; and whether it be not more prudent to prevent than to redress an evil?

23. Qu. Supposing there had been hitherto no such thing as a bank, and the question were now first proposed, whether it would be safer to circulate unlimited bills in a private credit, or bills to a limited value on the public credit of the community, what would men think?

24. Qu. Whether experience and example be not the plainest proof; and whether any instance can be assigned where a national bank hath not been attended with great advantage to the public?

25. Qu. Whether the evils apprehended from a national bank are not much more to be apprehended from private banks; but whether men by custom are not familiarized and reconciled to common dangers, which are therefore thought less than they really are?

26. Qu. Whether it would not be very hard to suppose all sense, honesty, and public spirit were in the keeping of only a few private men, and the public was not fit to be trusted?

27. Qu. Whether it be not ridiculous to suppose a legislature should be afraid to trust itself?

28. Qu. But, whether a private interest be not generally supported and pursued with more zeal than a public?

29. Qu. Whether the maxim, 'What is everybody's business is nobody's,' prevails in any country under the sun more than in Ireland?

30. Qu. Whether, nevertheless, the community of danger, which lulls private men asleep, ought not to awaken the public?

31. Qu. Whether there be not less security where there are more temptations and fewer checks?

32. Qu. If a man is to risk his fortune, whether it be more prudent to risk it on the credit of private men, or in that of the great assembly of the nation?

33. Qu. Where is it most reasonable to expect wise and punctual dealing, whether in a secret impenetrable recess, where credit

depends on secrecy, or in a public management regulated and inspected by Parliament?

34. Qu. Whether a supine security be not catching, and whether numbers running the same risk, as they lessen the caution, may not increase the danger?

35. Qu. What real objection lies against a national bank erected by the legislature, and in the management of public deputies, appointed and inspected by the legislature?

36. Qu. What have we to fear from such a bank, which may not be as well feared without it?

37. Qu. How, why, by what means, or for what end, should it become an instrument of oppression?

38. Qu. Whether we can possibly be on a more precarious foot than we are already? Whether it be not in the power of any particular person at once to disappear and convey himself into foreign parts? or whether there can be any security in an estate of land when the demands upon it are unknown?

39. Qu. Whether the establishing of a national bank, if we suppose a concurrence of the government, be not very practicable?

40. Qu. But, whether though a scheme be never so evidently practicable and useful to the pubic, yet, if conceived to interfere with a private interest, it be not forthwith in danger of appearing doubtful, difficult, and impracticable?

41. Qu. Whether the legislative body hath not already sufficient power to hurt, if they may be supposed capable of it, and whether a bank would give them any new power?

42. Qu. What should tempt the pubic to defraud itself?

43. Qu. Whether, if the legislature destroyed the public, it would not be felo de se; and whether it be reasonable to suppose it bent on its own destruction?

44. Qu. Whether the objection to a pubic national bank, from want of secrecy, be not in truth an argument for it?

45. Qu. Whether the secrecy of private banks be not the very thing that renders them so hazardous? and whether, without that, there could have been of late so many sufferers?

46. Qu. Whether when all objections are answered it be still incumbent to answer surmises?

47. Qu. Whether it were just to insinuate that gentlemen would be against any proposal they could not turn into a job?

48. Qu. Suppose the legislature passed their word for any private banker, and regularly visited his books, would not money lodged in his bank be therefore reckoned more secure?

49. Qu. In a country where the legislative body is not fit to be trusted, what security can there be for trusting any one else?

50. Qu. If it be not ridiculous to question whether the pubic can find cash to circulate bills of a limited value when private bankers are supposed to find enough to circulate them to an unlimited value?

51. Qu. Whether the united stock of a nation be not the best security? And whether anything but the ruin of the State can produce a national bankruptcy?

52. Qu. Whether the total sum of the public treasure, power, and wisdom, all co-operating, be not most likely to establish a bank of

credit, sufficient to answer the ends, relieve the wants, and satisfy the scruples of all people?

53. Qu. Whether those hazards that in a greater degree attend private banks can be admitted as objections against a public one?

54. Qu. Whether that which is an objection to everything be an objection to anything; and whether the possibility of an abuse be not of that kind?

55. Qu. Whether, in fact, all things are not more or less abused, and yet notwithstanding such abuse, whether many things are not upon the whole expedient and useful?

56. Qu. Whether those things that are subject to the most general inspection are not the least subject to abuse?

57. Qu. Whether, for private ends, it may not be sometimes expedient to object novelty to things that have been often tried, difficulty to the plainest things, and hazard to the safest?

58. Qu. Whether some men will not be apt to argue as if the question was between money and credit, and not (as in fact it is) which ought to be preferred, private credit or public credit?

59. Qu. Whether they will not prudently overlook the evils felt, or to be feared, on one side?

60. Qu. Whether, therefore, those that would make an impartial judgment ought not to be on their guard, keeping both prospects always in view, balancing the inconveniencies on each side and considering neither absolutely?

61. Qu. Whether wilful mistakes, examples without a likeness, and general addresses to the passions are not often more successful than arguments?

62. Qu. Whether there be not an art to puzzle plain cases as well as to explain obscure ones?

63. Qu. Whether private men are not often an over-match for the public; want of weight being made up for by activity?

64. Qu. If we suppose neither sense nor honesty in our leaders or representatives, whether we are not already undone, and so have nothing further to fear?

65. Qu. Suppose a power in the government to hurt the pubic by means of a national bank, yet what should give them the will to do this? Or supposing a will to do mischief, yet how could a national bank, modelled and administered by Parliament, put it in their power?

66. Qu. Whether even a wicked will entrusted with power can be supposed to abuse it for no end?

67. Qu. Whether it be not much more probable that those who maketh such objections do not believe them?

68. Qu. Whether it be not vain to object that our fellow-subjects of Great Britain would malign or obstruct our industry when it is exerted in a way which cannot interfere with their own?

66. Qu. Whether it is to be supposed they should take delight in the dirt and nakedness and famine of our people, or envy them shoes for their feet and beef for their belies?

70. Qu. What possible handle or inclination could our having a national bank give other people to distress us?

71. Qu. Whether it be not ridiculous to conceive that a project for cloathing and feeding our natives should give any umbrage to England?

72. Qu. Whether such unworthy surmises are not the pure effect of spleen?

73. Qu. Whether London is not to be considered as the metropolis of Ireland? And whether our wealth (such as it is) doth not circulate through London and throughout all England, as freely as that of any part of his Majesty's dominions?

74. Qu. Whether therefore it be not evidently the interest of the people of England to encourage rather than to oppose a national bank in this kingdom, as well as every other means for advancing our wealth which shall not impair their own?

75. Qu. Whether it is not our interest to be useful to them rather than rival them; and whether in that case we may not be sure of their good offices?

76. Qu. Whether we can propose to thrive so long as we entertain a wrongheaded distrust of England?

77. Qu. Whether, as a national bank would increase our industry, and that our wealth, England may not be a proportionable gainer; and whether we should not consider the gains of our mother-country as some accession to our own?

78. Qu. Whether the Protestant colony in this kingdom can ever forget what they owe to England?

79. Qu. Whether there ever was in any part of the world a country in such wretched circumstances, and which, at the same time, could be so easily remedied, and nevertheless the remedy not applied?

80. Qu. What must become of a people that can neither see the plainest things nor do the easiest?

81. Qu. Be the money lodged in the bank what it will, yet whether an Act to make good deficiencies would not remove all scruples?

82. Qu. If it be objected that a national bank must lower interest, and therefore hurt the monied man, whether the same objection would not hold as strong against multiplying our gold and silver?

83. Qu. But whether a bank that utters bills, with the sole view of promoting the public weal, may not so proportion their quantity as to avoid several inconveniencies which might attend private banks?

84. Qu. Whether there be any difficulty in comprehending that the whole wealth of the nation is in truth the stock of a national bank? And whether any more than the right comprehension of this be necessary to make all men easy with regard to its credit?

85. Qu. Whether any Thing be more reasonable than that the pubic, which makes the whole profit of the bank, should engage to make good its credit?

86. Qu. Whether the prejudices about gold and silver are not strong, but whether they are not still prejudices?

87. Qu. Whether paper doth not by its stamp and signature acquire a local value, and become as precious and as scarce as gold? And whether it be not much fitter to circulate large sums, and therefore preferable to gold?

88. Qu. Whether, in order to make men see and feel, it be not often necessary to inculcate the same thing, and place it in different lights?

89. Qu. Whether it doth not much import to have a right conception of money? And whether its true and just idea be not

that of a ticket, entitling to power, and fitted to record and transfer such power?

90. Qu. Whether the managers and officers of a national bank ought to be considered otherwise than as the cashiers and clerks of private banks? Whether they are not in effect as little trusted, have as little power, are as much limited by rules, and as liable to inspection?

91. Qu. Whether the mistaking this point may not create some prejudice against a national bank, as if it depended on the credit, or wisdom, or honesty, of private men, rather than on the pubic, which is really the sole proprietor and director thereof, and as such obliged to support it?

92. Qu. Though the bank of Amsterdam doth very rarely, if at all, pay out money, yet whether every man possess'd of specie be not ready to convert it into paper, and act as cashier to the bank? And whether, from the same motive, every monied man throughout this kingdom would not be cashier to our national bank?

93. Qu. Whether a national bank would not be the great means and motive for employing our poor in manufactures?

94. Qu. Whether money, though lent out only to the rich, would not soon circulate among the poor? And whether any man borrows but with an intent to circulate?

95. Qu. Whether both government and people would not in the event be gainers by a national bank? And whether anything but wrong conceptions of its nature can make those that wish well to either averse from it?

96. Qu. Whether it may not be right to think, and to have it thought, that England and Ireland, prince and people, have one and the same interest?

97. Qu. Whether, if we had more means to set on foot such manufactures and such commerce as consists with the interest of England, there would not of course be less sheep-walk, and less wool exported to foreign countries? And whether a national bank would not supply such means?

98. Qu. Whether we may not obtain that as friends which it is in vain to hope for as rivals?

99. Qu. Whether in every instance by which we prejudice England, we do not in a greater degree prejudice ourselves? See Part II. qu. 153 and 154.

100. Qu. Whether in the rude original of society the first step was not the exchanging of commodities; the next a substituting of metals by weight as the common medium of circulation; after this the making use of coin; lastly, a further refinement by the use of paper with proper marks and signatures? And whether this, as it is the last, so it be not the greatest improvement?

101. Qu. Whether we are not in fact the only people who may be said to starve in the midst of plenty?

102. Qu. Whether business in general doth not languish among us? Whether our land is not untilled? Whether its inhabitants are not upon the wing?

103. Qu. Whether there can be a worse sign than that people should quit their country for a livelihood? Though men often leave their country for health, or pleasure, or riches, yet to leave it merely for a livelihood, whether this be not exceeding bad, and sheweth some peculiar mismanagement?

104. Qu. Whether our circumstances do not call aloud for some present remedy? And whether that remedy be not in our power?

105. Qu. Whether, in order to redress our evils, artificial helps are not most wanted in a land where industry is most against the natural grain of the people?

106. Qu. Whether, of all the helps to industry that ever were invented, there be any more secure, more easy, and more effectual than a national bank?

107. Qu. Whether medicines do not recommend themselves by experience, even though their reasons be obscure? But whether reason and fact are not equally clear in favour of this political medicine?

108. Qu. Whether, although the prepossessions about gold and silver have taken deep root, yet the example of our Colonies in America doth not make it as plain as day-light that they are not so necessary to the wealth of a nation as the vulgar of all ranks imagine?

109. Qu. Whether it be not evident that we may maintain a much greater inward and outward commerce, and be five times richer than we are, nay, and our bills abroad be of far greater credit, though we had not one ounce of gold or silver in the whole island?

110. Qu. Whether wrongheaded maxims, customs, and fashions are not sufficient to destroy any people which hath so few resources as the inhabitants of Ireland.

111. Qu. Whether it would not be a horrible thing to see our matrons make dress and play their chief concern?

112. Qu. Whether our ladies might not as well endow monasteries as wear Flanders lace? And whether it be not true that Popish nuns are maintained by Protestant contributions?

113. Qu. Whether England, which hath a free trade, whatever she remits for foreign luxury with one hand, doth not with the other receive much more from abroad? Whether, nevertheless, this nation would not be a gainer, if our women would content themselves with the same moderation in point of expense as the English ladies?

114. Qu. But whether it be not a notorious truth that our Irish ladies are on a foot, as to dress, with those of five times their fortune in England?

115. Qu. Whether it be not even certain that the matrons of this forlorn country send out a greater proportion of its wealth, for fine apparel, than any other females on the whole surface of this terraqueous globe?

116. Qu. Whether the expense, great as it is, be the greatest evil; but whether this folly may not produce many other follies, an entire derangement of domestic life, absurd manners, neglect of duties, bad mothers, a general corruption in both sexes?

117. Qu. Whether therefore a tax on all gold and silver in apparel, on all foreign laces and silks, may not raise a fund for the bank, and at the same time have other salutary effects on the public?

118. Qu. But, if gentlemen had rather tax themselves in another way, whether an additional tax of ten shillings the hogshead on wines may not supply a sufficient fund for the national bank, all defects to be made good by Parliament?

119. Qu. Whether upon the whole it may not be right to appoint a national bank?

120. Qu. Whether the stock and security of such bank would not be, in truth, the national stock, or the total sum of the wealth of this kingdom?

121. Qu. Whether, nevertheless, there should not be a particular fund for present use in answering bills and circulating credit?

122. Qu. Whether for this end any fund may not suffice, provided an Act be passed for making good deficiencies?

123. Qu. Whether the sole proprietor of such bank should not be the public, and the sole director the legislature?

124. Qu. Whether the managers, officers, and cashiers should not be servants of the pubic, acting by orders and limited by rules of the legislature?

125. Qu. Whether there should not be a standing number of inspectors, one-third men in great office, the rest members of both houses, half whereof to go out, and half to come in every session?

126. Qu. Whether those inspectors should not, all in a body, visit twice a year, and three as often as they pleased?

127. Qu. Whether the general bank should not be in Dubin, and subordinate banks or compters one in each province of Munster, Ulster, and Connaught?

128. Qu. Whether there should not be such provisions of stamps, signatures, checks, strong boxes, and all other measures for securing the bank notes and cash, as are usual in other banks?

129. Qu. Whether these ten or a dozen last queries may not easily be converted into heads of a bill?

130. Qu. Whether any one concerns himself about the security or funds of the banks of Venice or Amsterdam? And whether in a little time the case would not be the same as to our bank?

131. Qu. Whether the first beginning of expedients do not always meet with prejudices? And whether even the prejudices of a people ought not to be respected?

132. Qu. Whether a national bank be not the true philosopher's stone in a State?

133. Qu. Whether it be not the most obvious remedy for all the inconveniencies we labour under with regard to our coin?

134. Qu. Whether it be not agreed on all hands that our coin is on very bad foot, and calls for some present remedy?

135. Qu. Whether the want of silver hath not introduced a sort of traffic for change, which is purchased at no inconsiderable discount to the great obstruction of our domestic commerce?

136. Qu. Whether, though it be evident silver is wanted, it be yet so evident which is the best way of providing for this want? Whether by lowering the gold, or raising the silver, or partly one, partly the other?

137. Qu. Whether a partial raising of one species be not, in truth, wanting a premium to our bankers for importing such species? And what that species is which deserves most to be encouraged?

138. Qu. Whether it be not just, that all gold should be alike rated according to its weight and fineness?

139. Qu. Whether this may be best done, by lowering some certain species of gold, or by raising others, or by joining both methods together?

140. Qu. Whether all regulations of coin should not be made with a view to encourage industry, and a circulation of commerce, throughout the kingdom?

141. Qu. Whether the North and the South have not, in truth, one and the same interest in this matter?

142. Qu. Whether to oil the wheels of commerce be not a common benefit? And whether this be not done by avoiding fractions and multiplying small silver?

143. Qu. But, whether a pubic benefit ought to be obtained by unjust methods, and therefore, whether any reduction of coin should be thought of which may hurt the properties of private men?

144. Qu. Whether those parts of the kingdom where commerce doth most abound would not be the greatest gainers by having our coin placed on a right foot?

145. Qu. Whether, in case a reduction of coin be thought expedient, the uttering of bank bills at the same time may not prevent the inconveniencies of such a reduction?

146. Qu. But, whether any pubic expediency could countervail a real pressure on those who are least able to bear it, tenants and debtors?

147. Qu. Whether, nevertheless, the political body, as well as the natural, must not sometimes be worse in order to be better?

148. Qu. Whether, all things considered, a general raising the value of gold and silver be not so far from bringing greater quantities thereof into the kingdom that it would produce a direct contrary effect, inasmuch as less, in that case, would serve, and

therefore less be wanted? And whether men do not import a commodity in proportion to the demand or want of it?

149. Qu. Whether the lowering of our gold would not create a fever in the State? And whether a fever be not sometimes a cure, but whether it be not the last cure a man would choose?

150. Qu. What if our other gold were raised to a par with Portugal gold, and the value of silver in general raised with regard to that of gold?

151. Qu. Whether the pubic ends may or may not be better answered by such augmentation, than by a reduction of our coin?

152. Qu. Provided silver is multiplied, be it by raising or diminishing the value of our coin, whether the great end is not answered?

153. Qu. Whether raising the value of a particular species will not tend to multiply such species, and to lessen others in proportion thereunto? And whether a much less quantity of cash in silver would not, in reality, enrich the nation more than a much greater in gold?

154. Qu. Whether, if a reduction be thought necessary, the obvious means to prevent all hardships and injustice be not a national bank?

155. Qu. Upon supposition that the cash of this kingdom was five hundred thousand pounds, and by lowering the various species each one-fifth of its value the whole sum was reduced to four hundred thousand pounds, whether the difficulty of getting money, and consequently of paying rents, would not be increased in the proportion of five to four?

156. Qu. Whether such difficulty would not be a great and unmerited distress on all the tenants in the nation? But if at the same time with the aforesaid reduction there were uttered one hundred thousand pounds additional to the former current stock, whether such difficulty or inconvenience would then be felt?

157. Qu. Whether, ceteris paribus, it be not true that the prices of things increase as the quantity of money increaseth, and are diminished as that is diminished? And whether, by the quantity of money is not to be understood the amount of the denominations, all contracts being nominal for pounds, shillings, and pence, and not for weights of gold or silver?

158. Qu. Whether in any foreign market, twopence advance in a kilderkin of corn could greatly affect our trade?

159. Qu. Whether in regard of the far greater changes and fluctuations of prices from the difference of seasons and other accidents, that small rise should seem considerable?

160. Qu. Whether our exports do not consist of such necessaries as other countries cannot well be without?

161. Qu. Whether upon the circulation of a national bank more land would not be tilled, more hands employed, and consequently more commodities exported?

162. Qu. Whether, setting aside the assistance of a national bank, it will be easy to reduce or lower our coin without some hardship (at least for the present) on a great number of particular persons?

163. Qu. Whether, nevertheless, the scheme of a national bank doth not entirely stand clear of this question; and whether such bank may not completely subsist and answer its ends, although there should be no alteration at all made in the value of our coin?

164. Qu. Whether, if the ill state of our coin be not redressed, that scheme would not be still more necessary, inasmuch as a national bank, by putting new life and vigour into our commerce, may prevent our feeling the ill effects of the want of such redress?

165. Qu. Whether men united by interest are not often divided by opinion; and whether such difference in opinion be not an effect of misapprehension?

166. Qu. Whether two things are not manifest, first, that some alteration in the value of our coin is highly expedient, secondly, that whatever alteration is made, the tenderest care should be had of the properties of the people, and even a regard paid to their prejudices?

167. Qu. Whether our taking the coin of another nation for more than it is worth be not, in reality and in event, a cheat upon ourselves?

168. Qu. Whether a particular coin over-rated will not be sure to flow in upon us from other countries beside that where it is coined?

169. Qu. Whether, in case the wisdom of the nation shall think fit to alter our coin, without erecting a national bank, the rule for lessening or avoiding present inconvenience should not be so to order matters, by raising the silver and depressing the gold, as that the total sum of coined cash within the kingdom shall, in denomination, remain the same, or amount to the same nominal value, after the change that it did before?

170. Qu. Whether all inconvenience ought not to be lessened as much as may be; but after, whether it would be prudent, for the sake of a small inconvenience, to obstruct a much greater good? And whether it may not sometimes happen that an inconvenience

which in fancy and general discourse seems great shall, when accurately inspected and cast up, appear inconsiderable?

171. Qu. Whether in public councils the sum of things, here and there, present and future, ought not to be regarded?

172. Qu. Whether silver and small money be not that which circulates the quickest, and passeth through all hands, on the road, in the market, at the shop?

173. Qu. Whether, all things considered, it would not be better for a kingdom that its cash consisted of half a million in small silver, than of five times that sum in gold?

174. Qu. Whether there be not every day five hundred lesser payments made for one that requires gold?

175. Qu. Whether Spain, where gold bears the highest value, be not the laziest, and China, where it bears the lowest, be not the most industrious country in the known world?

176. Qu. Money being a ticket which entitles to power and records the title, whether such power avails otherwise than as it is exerted into act?

177. Qu. Whether it be not evidently the interest of every State, that its money should rather circulate than stagnate?

178. Qu. Whether the principal use of cash be not its ready passing from hand to hand, to answer common occasions of the common people, and whether common occasions of all sorts of people are not small ones?

179. Qu. Whether business at fairs and markets is not often at a stand and often hindered, even though the seller hath his

commodities at hand and the purchaser his gold, yet for want of change?

180. Qu. Whether beside that value of money which is rated by weight, there be not also another value consisting in its aptness to circulate?

181. Qu. As wealth is really power, and coin a ticket conveying power, whether those tickets which are the fittest for that use ought not to be preferred?

182. Qu. Whether those tickets which singly transfer small shares of power, and, being multiplied, large shares, are not fitter for common use than those which singly transfer large shares?

183. Qu. Whether the public is not more benefited by a shilling that circulates than a pound that lies dead?

184. Qu. Whether sixpence twice paid be not as good as a shilling once paid?

185. Qu. Whether the same shilling circulating in a village may not supply one man with bread, another with stockings, a third with a knife, a fourth with paper, a fifth with nails, and so answer many wants which must otherwise have remained unsatisfied?

186. Qu. Whether facilitating and quickening the circulation of power to supply wants be not the promoting of wealth and industry among the lower people? And whether upon this the wealth of the great doth not depend?

187. Qu. Whether, without the proper means of circulation, it be not vain to hope for thriving manufacturers and a busy people?

188. Qu. Whether four pounds in small cash may not circulate and enliven an Irish market, which many four-pound pieces would permit to stagnate?

189. Qu. Whether a man that could move nothing less than a hundred-pound weight would not be much at a loss to supply his wants; and whether it would not be better for him to be less strong and more active?

190. Qu. Whether the natural body can be in a state of health and vigour without a due circulation of the extremities, even? And whether the political body, any in the fingers and toes more than the natural, can thrive without a proportionable circulation through the minutest and most inconsiderable parts thereof?

191. Qu. If we had a mint for coining only shillings, sixpences, and copper-money, whether the nation would not soon feel the good effects thereof?

192. Qu. Whether the greater waste by wearing of small coins would not be abundantly overbalanced by their usefulness?

193. Qu. Whether it be not the industry of common people that feeds the State, and whether it be possible to keep this industry alive without small money?

194. Qu. Whether the want of this be not a great bar to our employing the people in these manufactures which are open to us, and do not interfere with Great Britain?

195. Qu. Whether therefore such want doth not drive men into the lazy way of employing land under sheep-walk?

196. Qu. Whether the running of wool from Ireland can so effectually be prevented as by encouraging other business and manufactures among our people?

197. Qu. Whatever commodities Great Britain importeth which we might supply, whether it be not her real interest to import them from us rather than from any other people?

198. Qu. Whether the apprehension of many among us (who for that very reason stick to their wool), that England may hereafter prohibit, limit, or discourage our linen trade, when it hath been once, with great pains and expense, thoroughly introduced and settled in this land, be not altogether groundless and unjust?

199. Qu. Whether it is possible for this country, which hath neither mines of gold nor a free trade, to support for any time the sending out of specie?

200. Qu. Whether in fact our payments are not made by bills? And whether our foreign credit doth not depend on our domestic industry, and our bills on that credit?

201. Qu. Whether, in order to mend it, we ought not first to know the peculiar wretchedness of our state? And whether there be any knowing of this but by comparison?

202. Qu. Whether there are not single market towns in England that turn more money in buying and selling than whole counties (perhaps provinces) with us?

203. Qu. Whether the small town of Birmingham alone doth not, upon an average, circulate every week, one way or other, to the value of fifty thousand pounds? But whether the same crown may not be often paid?

204. Qu. Whether there be any woollen manufacture in Birmingham?

205. Qu. Whether bad management may not be worse than slavery? And whether any part of Christendom be in a more languishing condition than this kingdom?

206. Qu. Whether any kingdom in Europe be so good a customer at Bordeaux as Ireland?

207. Qu. Whether the police and economy of France be not governed by wise councils? And whether any one from this country, who sees their towns, and manufactures, and commerce, will not wonder what our senators have been doing?

208. Qu. What variety and number of excellent manufactures are to be met with throughout the whole kingdom of France?

209. Qu. Whether there are not everywhere some or other mills for many uses, forges and furnaces for iron-work, looms for tapestry, glass-houses, and so forth?

210. Qu. What quantities of paper, stockings, hats; what manufactures of wool, silk, linen, hemp, leather, wax, earthenware, brass, lead, tin, &c?

211. Qu. Whether the manufactures and commerce of the single town of Lyons do not amount to a greater value than all the manufactures and all the trade of this kingdom taken together?

212. Qu. Whether it be not true, that within the compass of one year there flowed from the South Sea, when that commerce was open, into the single town of St. Malo's, a sum in gold and silver equal to four times the whole specie of this kingdom? And whether that same part of France doth not at present draw from Cadiz, upwards of two hundred thousand pounds per annum?

213. Qu. Whether, in the anniversary fair at the small town of Beaucaire upon the Rhone, there be not as much money laid out as the current cash of this kingdom amounts to?

214. Qu. Whether it be true that the Dutch make ten millions of livres, every return of the flota and galleons, by their sales at the Indies and at Cadiz?

215. Qu. Whether it be true that England makes at least one hundred thousand pounds per annum by the single article of hats sold in Spain?

216. Qu. Whether the very shreds shorn from woollen cloth, which are thrown away in Ireland, do not make a beautiful tapestry in France?

217. Qu. Whether the toys of Thiers do not employ five thousand families?

218. Qu. Whether there be not a small town Or two in France which supply all Spain with cards?

219. Qu. Whether there be not French towns subsisted merely by making pins?

220. Qu. Whether the coarse fingers of those very women, those same peasants who one part of the year till the ground and dress the vineyards, are not another employed in making the finest French point?

221. Qu. Whether there is not a great number of idle fingers among the wives and daughters of our peasants?

222. Qu. Whether, about twenty-five years ago, they did not first attempt to make porcelain in France; and whether, in a few years,

they did not make it so well, as to rival that which comes from China?

223. Qu. Whether the French do not raise a trade from saffron, dyeing drugs, and the like products, which may do with us as well as with them?

224. Qu. Whether we may not have materials of our own growth to supply all manufactures, as well as France, except silk, and whether the bulk of what silk even France manufactures be not imported?

225. Qu. Whether it be possible for this country to grow rich, so long as what is made by domestic industry is spent in foreign luxury?

226. Qu. Whether part of the profits of the bank should not be employed in erecting manufactures of several kinds, which are not likely to be set on foot and carried on to perfection without great stock, public encouragement, general regulations, and the concurrence of many hands?

227. Qu. Whether our natural Irish are not partly Spaniards and partly Tartars, and whether they do not bear signatures of their descent from both these nations, which is also confirmed by all their histories?

228. Qu. Whether the Tartar progeny is not numerous in this land? And whether there is an idler occupation under the sun than to attend flocks and herds of cattle?

229. Qu. Whether the wisdom of the State should not wrestle with this hereditary disposition of our Tartars, and with a high hand introduce agriculture?

230. Qu. Whether it were not to be wished that our people shewed their descent from Spain, rather by their honour and honesty than their pride, and if so, whether they might not easily insinuate themselves into a larger share of the Spanish trade?

231. Qu. Whether once upon a time France did not, by her linen alone, draw yearly from Spain about eight millions of livres?

232. Qu. Whether the French have not suffered in their linen trade with Spain, by not making their cloth of due breadth; and whether any other people have suffered, and are still likely to suffer, through the same prevarication?

233. Qu. Whether the Spaniards are not rich and lazy, and whether they have not a particular inclination and favour for the inhabitants of this island? But whether a punctual people do not love punctual dealers?

234. Qu. Whether about fourteen years ago we had not come into a considerable share of the linen trade with Spain, and what put a stop to this?

235. Qu. Whether we may not, with common industry and common honesty, undersell any nation in Europe?

236. Qu. Whether, if the linen manufacture were carried on in the other provinces as well as in the North, the merchants of Cork, Limerick, and Galway would not soon find the way to Spain?

237. Qu. Whether the woollen manufacture of England is not divided into several parts or branches, appropriated to particular places, where they are only or principally manufactured; fine cloths in Somersetshire, coarse in Yorkshire, long ells at Exeter, saies at Sudbury, crapes at Norwich, linseys at Kendal, blankets at Witney, and so forth?

238. Qu. Whether the united skill, industry, and emulation of many together on the same work be not the way to advance it? And whether it had been otherwise possible for England to have carried on her woollen manufacture to so great perfection?

239. Qu. Whether it would not on many accounts be right if we observed the same course with respect to our linen manufacture; and that diapers were made in one town or district, damasks in another, sheeting in a third, fine wearing linen in a fourth, coarse in a fifth, in another cambrics, in another thread and stockings, in others stamped linen, or striped linen, or tickings, or dyed linen, of which last kinds there is so great a consumption among the seafaring men of all nations?

240. Qu. Whether it may not be worth while to inform ourselves of the different sorts of linen which are in request among different people?

241. Qu. Whether we do not yearly consume of French wines about a thousand tuns more than either Sweden or Denmark, and yet whether those nations pay ready money as we do?

242. Qu. Whether they are not the Swiss that make hay and gather in the harvest throughout Alsatia?

243. Qu. Whether it be not a custom for some thousands of Frenchmen to go about the beginning of March into Spain, and having tilled the lands and gathered the harvest of Spain, to return home with money in their pockets about the end of November?

244. Qu. Whether of late years our Irish labourers do not carry on the same business in England to the great discontent of many there? But whether we have not much more reason than the people of England to be displeased at this commerce?

245. Qu. Whether, notwithstanding the cash supposed to be brought into it, any nation is, in truth, a gainer by such traffic?

246. Qu. Whether the industry of our people employed in foreign lands, while our own are left uncultivated, be not a great loss to the country?

247. Qu. Whether it would not be much better for us, if, instead of sending our men abroad, we could draw men from the neighbouring countries to cultivate our own?

248. Qu. Whether, nevertheless, we are not apt to think the money imported by our labourers to be so much clear gains to this country, but whether a little reflexion and a little political arithmetic may not shew us our mistake?

249. Qu. Whether our prejudices about gold and silver are not very apt to infect or misguide our judgments and reasonings about the public weal?

250. Qu. Whether it be not a good rule whereby to judge of the trade of any city, and its usefulness, to observe whether there is a circulation through the extremities, and whether the people round about are busy and warm?

251. Qu. Whether we had not, some years since, a manufacture of hats at Athlone, and of earthenware at Arklow, and what became of those manufactures?

252. Qu. Why we do not make tiles of our own, for flooring and roofing, rather than bring them from Holland?

253. Qu. What manufactures are there in France and Venice of gilt-leather, how cheap and how splendid a furniture?

254. Qu. Whether we may not, for the same use, manufacture divers things at home of more beauty and variety than wainscot, which is imported at such expense from Norway?

255. Qu. Whether the use and the fashion will not soon make a manufacture?

256. Qu. Whether, if our gentry used to drink mead and cider, we should not soon have those liquors in the utmost perfection and plenty?

257. Qu. Whether it be not wonderful that with such pastures, and so many black cattle, we do not find ourselves in cheese?

258. Qu. Whether great profits may not be made by fisheries; but whether those of our Irish who live by that business do not contrive to be drunk and unemployed one half of the year?

259. Qu. Whether it be not folly to think an inward commerce cannot enrich a State, because it doth not increase its quantity of gold and silver? And whether it is possible a country should? not thrive, while wants are supplied, and business goes on?

260. Qu. Whether plenty of all the necessaries and comforts of life be not real wealth?

261. Qu. Whether Lyons, by the advantage of her midland situation and the rivers Rhone and Saone, be not a great magazine or mart for inward commerce? And whether she doth not maintain a constant trade with most parts of France; with Provence for oils and dried fruits, for wines and cloth with Languedoc, for stuffs with Champagne, for linen with Picardy, Normandy, and Brittany, for corn with Burgundy?

262. Qu. Whether she doth not receive and utter all those commodities, and raise a profit from the distribution thereof, as

well as of her own manufactures, throughout the kingdom of France?

263. Qu. Whether the charge of making good roads and navigable rivers across the country would not be really repaid by an inward commerce?

264. Qu. Whether, as our trade and manufactures increased, magazines should not be established in proper places, fitted by their situation, near great roads and navigable rivers, lakes, or canals, for the ready reception and distribution of all sorts of commodities from and to the several parts of the kingdom; and whether the town of Athlone, for instance, may not be fitly situated for such a magazine, or centre of domestic commerce?

265. Qu. Whether an inward trade would not cause industry to flourish, and multiply the circulation of our coin, and whether this may not do as well as multiplying the coin itself?

266. Qu. Whether the benefits of a domestic commerce are sufficiently understood and attended to; and whether the cause thereof be not the prejudiced and narrow way of thinking about gold and silver?

267. Qu. Whether there be any other more easy and unenvied method of increasing the wealth of a people?

268. Qu. Whether we of this island are not from our peculiar circumstances determined to this very commerce above any other, from the number of necessaries and good things that we possess within ourselves, from the extent and variety of our soil, from the navigable rivers and good roads which we have or may have, at a less expense than any people in Europe, from our great plenty of materials for manufactures, and particularly from the restraints we lie under with regard to our foreign trade?

269. Qu. Whether commissioners of trade or other proper persons should not be appointed to draw up plans of our commerce both foreign and domestic, and lay them at the beginning of every session before the Parliament?

270. Qu. Whether registers of industry should not be kept, and the pubic from time to time acquainted what new manufactures are introduced, what increase or decrease of old ones?

271. Qu. Whether annual inventories should not be published of the fairs throughout the kingdom, in order to judge of the growth of its commerce?

272. Qu. Whether there be not every year more cash circulated at the card tables of Dublin than at all the fairs of Ireland?

273. Qu. Whether the wealth of a country will not bear proportion to the skill and industry of its inhabitants?

274. Qu. Whether foreign imports that tend to promote industry should not be encouraged, and such as have a tendency to promote luxury should not be discouraged?

275. Qu. Whether the annual balance of trade between Italy and Lyons be not about four millions in favour of the former, and yet, whether Lyons be not a gainer by this trade?

276. Qu. Whether the general rule, of determining the profit of a commerce by its balance, doth not, like other general rules, admit of exceptions?

277. Qu. Whether it would not be a monstrous folly to import nothing but gold and silver, supposing we might do it, from every foreign part to which we trade? And yet, whether some men may not think this foolish circumstance a very happy one?

278. Qu. But whether we do not all see the ridicule of the Mogul's subjects, who take from us nothing but our silver, and bury it under ground, in order to make sure thereof against the resurrection?

279. Qu. Whether he must not be a wrongheaded patriot or politician, whose ultimate view was drawing money into a country, and keeping it there?

280. Qu. Whether it be not evident that not gold but industry causeth a country to flourish?

281. Qu. Whether it would not be a silly project in any nation to hope to grow rich by prohibiting the exportation of gold and silver?

282. Qu. Whether there can be a greater mistake in politics than to measure the wealth of the nation by its gold and silver?

283. Qu. Whether gold and silver be not a drug, where they do not promote industry? Whether they be not even the bane and undoing of an idle people?

284. Qu. Whether gold will not cause either industry or vice to flourish? And whether a country, where it flowed in without labour, must not be wretched and dissolute like an island inhabited by buccaneers?

285. Qu. Whether arts and vertue are not likely to thrive, where money is made a means to industry? But whether money without this would be a blessing to any people?

286. Qu. Whether therefore Mississippi, South Sea, and such like schemes were not calculated for pubic ruin?

287. Qu. Whether keeping cash at home, or sending it abroad, just as it most serves to promote industry, be not the real interest of every nation?

288. Qu. Whether commodities of all kinds do not naturally flow where there is the greatest demand? Whether the greatest demand for a thing be not where it is of most use? Whether money, like other things, hath not its proper use? Whether this use be not to circulate? Whether therefore there must not of course be money where there is a circulation of industry?

289. Qu. Whether all such princes and statesmen are not greatly deceived who imagine that gold and silver, any way got, will enrich a country?

290. Qu. Whether it is not a great point to know what we would be at? And whether whole States, as well as private persons, do not often fluctuate for want of this knowledge?

291. Qu. Whether gold may not be compared to Sejanus's horse, if we consider its passage through the world, and the fate of those nations which have been successively possess'd thereof?

292. Qu. Whether the effect is not to be considered more than the kind or quantity of money?

293. Qu. Whether means are not so far useful as they answer the end? And whether, in different circumstances, the same ends are not obtained by different means?

294. Qu. If we are a poor nation, abounding with very poor people, will it not follow that a far greater proportion of our stock should be in the smallest and lowest species than would suit with England?

295. Qu. Whether, therefore, it would not be highly expedient if our money were coined of peculiar values, best fitted to the circumstances and uses of our own country; and whether any other people could take umbrage at our consulting our own convenience, in an affair entirely domestic, and that lies within ourselves?

296. Qu. Whether every man doth not know, and hath not long known, that the want of a mint causeth many other wants in this kingdom?

297. Qu. What harm did England sustain about three centuries ago, when silver was coined in this kingdom?

298. Qu. What harm was it to Spain that her provinces of Naples and Sicily had all along mints of their own?

299. Qu. Whether those who have the interests of this kingdom at heart, and are concerned in the councils thereof, ought not to make the most humble and earnest representations to his Majesty, that he may vouchsafe to grant us that favour, the want of which is ruinous to our domestic industry, and the having of which would interfere with no interest of our fellow-subjects?

300. Qu. Whether it may not be presumed that our not having a privilege which every other kingdom in the world enjoys, be not owing to our want of diligence and unanimity in soliciting for it?

301. Qu. Whether his most gracious Majesty hath ever been addressed on this head in a proper manner, and had the case fairly stated for his royal consideration, and if not, whether we may not blame ourselves?

302. Qu. If his Majesty would be pleased to grant us a mint, whether the consequences thereof may not prove a valuable consideration to the crown?

303. Qu. Whether it be not the interest of England that we should cultivate a domestic commerce among ourselves? And whether it could give them any possible jealousy, if our small sum of cash was contrived to go a little further, if there was a little more life in our markets, a little more buying and selling in our shops, a little better provision for the backs and bellies of so many forlorn wretches throughout the towns and villages of this island?

304. Qu. Whether Great Britain ought not to promote the prosperity of her Colonies, by all methods consistent with her own? And whether the Colonies themselves ought to wish or aim at it by others?

305. Qu. Whether the remotest parts from the metropolis, and the lowest of the people, are not to be regarded as the extremities and capillaries of the political body?

306. Qu. Whether, although the capillary vessels are small, yet obstructions in them do not produce great chronical diseases?

307. Qu. Whether faculties are not enlarged and improved by exercise?

308. Qu. Whether the sum of the faculties put into act, or, in other words, the united action of a whole people, doth not constitute the momentum of a State?

309. Qu. Whether such momentum be not the real stock or wealth of a State; and whether its credit be not proportional thereunto?

310. Qu. Whether in every wise State the faculties of the mind are not most considered?

311. Qu. Whether every kind of employment or business, as it implies more skill and exercise of the higher powers, be not more valued?

312. Qu. Whether the momentum of a State doth not imply the whole exertion of its faculties, intellectual and corporeal; and whether the latter without the former could act in concert?

313. Qu. Whether the divided force of men, acting singly, would not be a rope of sand?

314. Qu. Whether the particular motions of the members of a State, in opposite directions, will not destroy each other, and lessen the momentum of the whole; but whether they must not conspire to produce a great effect?

315. Qu. Whether the ready means to put spirit into this State, to fortify and increase its momentum, would not be a national bank, and plenty of small cash?

316. Qu. Whether private endeavours without assistance from the public are likely to advance our manufactures and commerce to any great degree? But whether, as bills uttered from a national bank upon private mortgages would facilitate the purchases and projects of private men, even so the same bills uttered on the public security alone may not answer pubic ends in promoting new works and manufactures throughout the kingdom?

317. Qu. Whether that which employs and exerts the force of a community deserves not to be well considered and well understood?

318. Qu. Whether the immediate mover, the blood and spirits, be not money, paper, or metal; and whether the soul or will of the community, which is the prime mover that governs and directs the whole, be not the legislature?

319. Qu. Supposing the inhabitants of a country quite sunk in sloth, or even fast asleep, whether, upon the gradual awakening and exertion, first of the sensitive and locomotive faculties, next of reason and reflexion, then of justice and piety, the momentum of such country or State would not, in proportion thereunto, become still more and more considerable?

320. Qu. Whether that which in the growth is last attained, and is the finishing perfection of a people, be not the first thing lost in their declension?

321. Qu. Whether force be not of consequence, as it is exerted; and whether great force without great wisdom may not be a nuisance?

322. Qu. Whether the force of a child, applied with art, may not produce greater effects than that of a giant? And whether a small stock in the hands of a wise State may not go further, and produce more considerable effects, than immense sums in the hands of a foolish one?

323. Qu. Whether as many as wish well to their country ought not to aim at increasing its momentum?

324. Qu. Whose fault is it if poor Ireland still continues poor?

www.ingramcontent.com/pod-product-compliance
Lightning Source LLC
Chambersburg PA
CBHW072201100426
42738CB00011BA/2497